KING JOHN

The true story of **John Charles** Leeds United Legend

by **Richard Coomber**

KING JOHN

The true story of **John Charles** Leeds United Legend

First published 2000
Leeds United Publishing Limited
Elland Road, Leeds
LS11 0ES

No part of this may be reproduced or used in any forms by means
of graphic, electronic or mechanical including recording, taping or
information storage or retrieval systems - without prior permission
in writing from Leeds United Publishing Limited.

ISBN 1 903415 00 4

A catalogue record is available for this book from the British
Library

Typeset and printed by Polar Print Group, Leicester

All photographs credited where possible

Acknowledgements

Maybe it's entering the back-nine of life, but I find myself becoming increasingly irritated when I listen to discussions about football that suggest nothing much counts before the arrival of the Premier League.

When Manchester United fans vote for Eric Cantona as their player of the century, way ahead of George Best, Bobby Charlton and Denis Law, I wonder if the game will ever be put in perspective again.

When youngsters look puzzled when you mention the names of Bobby Moore, Danny Blanchflower and Johnny Haynes, and witheringly dismiss players like Nat Lofthouse, Tom Finney and Stanley Matthews as old guys who played in baggy shorts, I want to weep.

What chance have Dixie Dean, Wilf Mannion, Alex James or even older great players got? And Ferenc Puskas, Alfredo di Stefano and Lev Yashin have no hope of recognition from a public who think all foreigners start at Chelsea.

Hopefully, one day, football fans will want to know a bit more about the wonderful players of the past, and when they do, John Charles will surely be one of the names they will come to revere.

I never saw John play but as a small kid in a Sussex village I grew up reading about him in my football annuals, seeing pictures of this Colossus in my dad's Daily Mirror, and hearing about his feats as I strained to hear Sports Report on an accumulator-driven wireless.

I knew he must be special. And as I've grown older and talked to people who did have the luck to see him, they confirmed every picture I had in my mind's eye.

That's why it has been such a joy to work on this small tribute to John.

It may be a slim volume but there are a lot of people to be thanked for helping me put it together. Firstly of course John, himself, who patiently sat and answered all the questions I put to him.

Jimmy Armfield, Barry Foster, John Helm, Cliff Jones, Ken Jones, Cliff Morgan, John Morgan, Michael Parkinson, Harold Williams and Kenneth Wolstenholme have generously shared their memories and thoughts with me.

I have drawn extensively on the files of the Yorkshire Post and Yorkshire Evening Post, and I am grateful to Tony Watson, the editor of the Yorkshire Post, for allowing me to reproduce the contemporary match reports, which give such a vivid picture of how John was seen while he was playing. I'd also like to acknowledge the Independent, who generously allowed me to reproduce Ken Jones's excellent tribute first published on John's 65th birthday.

Alwyn Fisher, a Leeds United fan for many years, kindly let me borrow his copy of John's first autobiography King of Soccer, which includes a picture of John in the back of the Elland Road net and a small, anxious boy leaning over the wall, ringed and marked 'Me, Easter 1957'.

Neil Howson of Leeds United Publishing managed to find a copy of John's other book, The Gentle Giant, which was published when he returned from Italy. Both were 'ghosted' by Kenneth Wolstenholme and I couldn't have written this book without them. Also very useful was Mario Risoli's recent book 'When Pele Broke Our Hearts - Wales and the 1958 World Cup'(Ashley Drake Publishing).

Polar Print Group have done their usual outstanding production job, while Neil Howson, Michelle Chaplin, Rachel Ogden and the rest of the people at Leeds United have done a great job of putting it on sale.

The responsibility for any errors is all my own.

Richard Coomber
March 2000

King John Contents

FOREWORD

By **Michael Parkinson**

The months leading up to the millennium produced a lot of lists which were supposed to contain the best at almost every subject under the sun.

I was invited to contribute to some of these and whenever I was asked about the greatest British footballers, I always said there were three players I honestly couldn't separate unless I was put before a firing squad.

The three best British footballers I ever saw were George Best, Tom Finney and John Charles.

The reasons were the same for all of them. Firstly, they could play anywhere on the field. They could probably play any position better than the people in their team who filled it.

Secondly - you might find an argument about George on this but I believe it firmly - they all played the game in the right spirit. They were great entertainers but they were also great sportsmen. They never sold the public short and had exemplary gifts.

John Charles was the complete footballer. In Italy they would play him up front until he scored, then switch him to centre-half to stop the other side scoring. That seems to me to be the perfect all rounder.

He's also such a good man and when people like Ian Wright get an honours award and John's never been recognised, you have to worry about politicians. If they get that wrong, what else can they get wrong?

I first saw John play when I went to Elland Road to see Barnsley take on Leeds, who had those wonderful blue and gold quartered shirts in those days.

We had a centre-forward at the time called Cecil McCormack, who broke every Barnsley record in his first season, and the big test was always going to be John Charles.

John put our wee man in his pocket for 89 minutes, then in the 90th Cecil got a chance and scored. So honours were just about even.

Even as a purblind Barnsley supporter, I thought John was a fantastic player. He was a star. You couldn't take your eyes off him on the field. I thought that if he'd been in our team, we'd have won every cup there was.

I'd never met John but by 1974 or so, I'd been doing the talk show and was invited to go and judge a Miss Britain contest at Jolly's night club in Stoke on Trent. Terrible job, but you understand it was for charity! I was standing at the bar thinking 'What am I doing here?' when there was a tap on my shoulder.

It was John. He said to me: 'You don't know me. My name's John Charles.'

I replied: `I don't know you? Are you bloody mad. You're my hero.'

He wasn't being affected. He was just being his usual modest self. He's a wonderful man. I adore him.

John Charles - a Colossus in the old gold and blue of Leeds United

EARLY DAYS

Major Buckley was chatting with local journalist Phil Brown under the main stand at Elland Road, when the Leeds United manager spotted two groundstaff boys sweeping up.

"You two," barked Buckley in his best parade ground voice, "come over here."

The lads shuffled over, clearly nervous, wondering if they had crossed the formidable Major. But they weren't in for one of his famous rollickings, rather he wanted to mark Brown's card that these were two players to look out for in the future.

"This is Grenville Hair," he said. "With a bit of luck he'll play full-back for England. And this," he added, pointing to the other tall, slim lad, "He'll play centre-half for Wales and won't need any luck. He'll be the best centre-half since Cullis."

Grenville Hair played nearly 500 times for Leeds United but didn't quite make the England side. The nearest he came were FA tours to the West Indies, Nigeria and Ghana, and New Zealand.

The other lad more than lived up to the Major's 1948 expectations. His name was John Charles. He not only eclipsed the great Wolves and England stopper Stan Cullis, but most other footballers in the world before or since.

The vastly experienced and much respected sportswriter Ken Jones is clear where John comes in the footballing firmament. He said: "The words 'world class' are bandied about too easily these days, but they certainly apply to John Charles. When I'm asked to name the greatest players of all time, I always say: Pele, Di Stefano, Puskas, Charles, Best, Maradona, Cruyff, Beckenbauer and perhaps Matthews."

Tom Holley, who was the Leeds centre-half supplanted by 17-year-old Charles, later became a journalist and recalled praise from England's top centre-forward and centre-half of the time. He wrote: "Nat Lofthouse was asked who was the best centre-half he had played against and without hesitation named John Charles. The same week Billy Wright was asked who was the greatest centre forward he had faced, and he again answered John Charles."

On many occasions John has been voted in the world's top ten; in 1997 he was voted the greatest overseas player to pull on a Juventus shirt; and he has the distinction of being one of only three non Italian players - the others were Michel Platini and Brian Laudrup - to be voted Italian footballer of the year.

William John Charles was born in Swansea on 27 December 1931, the second child and first son of

Younger brother Mel

Edward, known as Ned, a steel erector and useful amateur half-back, and his wife Lillian. They already had a daughter, Maureen, and later came two more sons Mel, who also became an international footballer, and Malcolm, and a second daughter Avril.

John attended Cwymdu Junior School until the age of 11, then moved on to Manselton Senior School by which time he was already a keen footballer. Encouraged by his dad, and inspired by his Swansea Town idol Roy Paul, John played wherever and whenever he could.

Swansea was a football town - a whole host of big names were to come out of the town over the next few years, including Trevor Ford, Cliff Jones, the Allchurch brothers Ivor and Len, and the outstanding Arsenal goalkeeper Jack Kelsey.

Indeed, Welsh football was about to enter arguably its most successful period over the next ten years, with Cardiff in the top flight and Swansea establishing themselves as a strong Second Division side. Even Newport County were holding their own in the Third Division South and enjoyed some moments of glory, like their 3-1 giant-killing FA Cup win over Leeds United in 1949. It was a wonderful time to grow up for a kid to whom the game's basic skills came naturally and fluently, with no formal coaching.

John recalled: "There was a park about two streets over from where we lived and we would play there all the time. It would start with three against three and gradually more and more kids would join in until it was usually about twenty against twenty!"

He was soon picked for the Manselton school team and at the age of 12 won a place in Swansea Boys' team. Alongside him was a young inside forward, Terry Medwin, who was to go on to play on the wing for Spurs and join John in the national team. Swansea Boys reached the quarter final of the English Schools Trophy, where they were knocked out by Leicester, drawing 1-1 at Swansea before going down 2-0 in the replay in Leicester, John's first trip outside his home town.

He left school at 14. With the steel industry booming, the odds were that his father would arrange an apprenticeship for the youngster, but such a course never had a chance because Swansea Town offered him a place on the groundstaff.

This was a million miles from the modern-day Premiership academies with their phalanx of coaches and physios, organised leagues, top class accommodation and education courses. In the late 1940s being on the groundstaff meant being a club dogsbody, as John described in his first autobiography 'King of Soccer': "Nearly all the clubs take on as many promising youngsters as they can and put them to work on the ground. It is impossible for them to sign as professionals until they are seventeen, so these youngsters spend their time doing any odd job around the ground. They weed the pitch, sweep the terraces, help to keep the dressing-rooms clean and tidy, help to look after the boots of the senior players, and generally make themselves useful. It is hard work, but for a lad desperately interested in the game, it is enjoyable work...The really keen boy can pick up a host of tips simply by keeping his eyes and ears open, and even the back-breaking job of weeding becomes pleasant if you dream of the future - of playing for Swansea Town and Wales."

I Remember John

Jimmy Armfield

JIMMY ARMFIELD has been at the top of football as a player, manager and administrator. A classy fullback, Jimmy played 568 league games for Blackpool and won 45 caps for England. He was part of the triumphant 1966 World Cup squad and went on to skipper his country. After hanging up his boots, 'Gentleman Jim' became manager of Bolton and Leeds United. He's had a successful career as a journalist and broadcaster, and in recent years became kingmaker at the Football Association when he was called in to advise on the appointments of England managers after the downfall of Graham Taylor.

Jimmy still has vivid memories of the first time he came across John Charles:

"My first memory of John is when we played Leeds at Elland Road over Christmas in 1956. It was just after their stand burned down and I don't think we would have played if Leeds hadn't needed the money so badly.

It was snowing and we took four hours to get there. There was no motorway in those days and we used to go via Burnley and Keighley.

The ground was white and the ball was orange. We lost 5-0 which was a big blow to us. John played centre forward and headed two of the goals. In those days they had Meek and Overfield on the wings and they used to just cross the ball from anywhere for him to head it.

I remember looking at John and thinking 'Flipping heck!' I went up with him at one of the goals and I ended up heading his chest. He was so big and had such a terrific leap.

I also played against him in internationals once or twice and I remember down at Cardiff he propped Wales up. We beat them, but if it hadn't been for John, goodness knows how many we would have scored.

When I was manager at Leeds, John used to come in quite a lot and I liked having him there. He's such a big amiable devil, nobody could dislike him. He's got no edge to him. He's still the same lad who came out of Swansea without a coat.

He was the same as a player. Even though he was big and powerful, he didn't foul people. That was the attraction of him.

"I remember looking at John and thinking 'Flipping heck!'."

I remember him telling me a story when I interviewed him for a radio programme on football legends. He told me that when Major Buckley moved him to centre forward, he scored a hat-trick. The following Monday when he arrived at the ground, the press and photographers were waiting there to see this new hero. The Leeds chairman was also there and he put his arm around John and said: 'John for every one of those goals, you can go to my garage and put a gallon of petrol in your car.' John replied: 'Thanks, Mr Chairman, but I haven't got a car.'

The first thing I think of when I think of John Charles is that he is the only British player who went to Italy and really made it. They still love him there."

go because I didn't have a passport! Dad had heard about Major Buckley and thought it would be a good opportunity for me. I don't think I would have gone on my own but Leeds also invited Bobby Hennings and Harry Griffiths, so it was agreed I would go and see what they had to say."

It was a long, confusing train trip for a lad who wasn't even sure where Leeds was, and at the end of it he was confronted by a fearsome figure.

Franklin Charles Buckley had been brought to Leeds United by the new chairman, Sam Bolton. It was something of a coup and a sure signal that Bolton meant business when he said he was going to revive the fortunes of a club whose results had been unimpressive since being relegated from the First Division immediately after the War.

The Major - he earned his rank in the First World War having also served in the Boer War - was 64 years old and brought with him a reputation as a disciplinarian who was not afraid to try new ideas and was particularly adept at spotting youthful talent.

Another big difference from the modern set-up, was that footballers were cheap, so clubs signed staffs so big even the richest clubs today would envy them. There were usually at least three teams packed with senior professionals, so the chances for a youngster to break through were slim. Although Swansea felt young John had a bright future, they never played him in the first team and he turned out only a couple of times in the reserves. Most of his matches were in the A team, in the local league, and it was while playing there that he was spotted by a man who was to change his life.

Jack Pickard was Leeds United's scout in south Wales and when he saw John playing in the local park, he immediately alerted Major Buckley, a man renowned for taking a chance with youngsters. Because John was still too young to sign pro forms, there was no way Swansea could stop him moving - and while Leeds were not one of the biggest clubs in the league at that stage, the fact that Buckley was their manager gave them a lot of clout.

John recalled: "Mr Pickard approached me to go for a trial at Leeds. He came round the house to see my parents and at first my mam said I couldn't

The archives of the Yorkshire Post newspaper provide us with some lively contemporary accounts of John's career through the eyes of the local correspondents.

Of particular interest are the stories of Richard (Dick) Ulyatt, the well respected sports editor of the paper, who followed John's career from his first appearance in a friendly against Queen of the South, to his final match before leaving for Juventus.

Along with Ronald Crowther of the now defunct Yorkshire Evening News, Dick Ulyatt was among the first to recognise the talent he was witnessing.

Our first report is of a match played on 23 April 1949. It was an end of season affair, completely unremarkable except that Major Buckley had decided that the young Welshman had done enough against Queen of the South to deserve his league debut. It earned him his first headline.

After spells as manager at then non-league Norwich City, and Blackpool, he took charge at Wolverhampton Wanderers from 1927 to 1944, lifting them from Second Division strugglers to runners up in the First Division and FA Cup finalists. He moved from there to Notts County and then on to Hull City before linking up with Leeds. His influence on his former clubs was still being felt for some time after his departure. All but three of Wolves' 1949 FA Cup winning side were 'Buckley Boys', as were six of Hull's promotion team that year, and on 16 March 1951, another of his finds, Jackie Sewell, broke the British transfer record when Sheffield Wednesday paid Notts County £34,000 for his services.

Buckley Boys were a recognised group several years before the Busby Babes shot to fame. "You know my method," Buckley told one journalist, "I believe in getting them young. These fancy prices are no good."

His methods were certainly idosyncratic at times. At Wolves he gave the players a monkey gland supplement because he thought it would sharpen their thinking. There, and later at Leeds, he paired players up on the halfway line and made them dance to music played over the tannoy system to improve their footwork. Indeed the loudspeakers played a big part in his methods. At Elland Road he would sit in the stand and bark out orders over the PA system during training, his industrial language producing a number of complaints from ladies living in the area.

One of Buckley's favourite sayings was: "I don't care how good a player is, if he can only kick with one foot, he's only half a footballer." It was a philosophy that produced an immediate shock for the nervous young hopeful from Swansea, who had played all his football at left half. For John's trial the Major wanted him to play right back.

John was nervous but reports: "I must have done well because after the match the Major told me he was satisfied and that he would like me to join the Leeds United groundstaff. He promised to find me

YORKSHIRE POST

MORNING EDITION   THE PRIDE OF YORKSHIRE   23RD APRIL 1949

| Blackburn Rovers | 0 |
| Leeds United | 0 |

Charles's Fine Form

by RICHARD ULYATT

Both Blackburn Rovers and Leeds United showed signs of post-Easter fatigue. The first half was reasonably good and was evenly fought. United could always pull out a counter-attack, Rudd and Iggleden working well on the left wing, but it was another story after half time.

Rovers had a greater share of the game but despite several forward line switches they could not produce a goal.

Scarson, United's goal-keeper, was sound when Blackburn, with inside left McLelland as chief marksman, did get in a shot, but much of Blackburn's approach work broke down in United's penalty area against the solid defence of Bannister and Milburn with sturdy aid from McCabe, Charles and Burden, United's half backs.

This game was 17-year-old Charles's Football League debut.

He held Blackburn's reserve centre forward, Fenton, and Fenton's second half deputy Priday, showing accuracy of kick, tackle and heading. There could be nothing but satisfaction for United in the boy's form.

Rovers centre half Pryde, more than twice as old as Charles, was also a valuable man. He had in front of him a fine wing half in Baldwin and alongside, a determined left back in Eckersley.

I Remember John

JOHN HELM is one of the most respected TV sports commentators of recent years. He has covered football all over the world including several World Cups. Here he recalls how as a boy in Baildon he made a special effort to see John Charles in action:

"I was twelve or thirteen at the time and supported Bradford Park Avenue. I'd heard about this magical man John Charles and when Park Avenue were away one day, I thought 'Right, I'm going to go and see the fella.'

I had to walk about three miles down to Shipley station, get a train and then a bus to Elland Road.

I'll never ever forget the day. Leeds were playing Portsmouth, they won 4-1 and John scored one of the best goals I've ever seen in my life.

He scored with what seemed to me to be a header from 30 yards out. It was an absolute bullet, and I was behind the goal that he headed the ball into.

I'll never forget it. It went in with such ferocious power. I can still see it in my mind's eye today.

It used to be thrilling for me when I watched Park Avenue and I thought they were all wonderful, but then I saw this man John Charles and he was just something else.

The man was a Colossus. He scored two that day and it was well worth the journey. I was in awe of him from then on."

good 'digs' and to give me all the coaching I required. He kept both promises.

"He didn't do much coaching on the training field. Instead he would call me into his office after a match and say: 'Jack - he always called me Jack, not John - you shouldn't have done so and so.' But he'd also tell me what I'd done right and suggest one or two things I might like to try. I would think about what he said and try to do it in matches."

Henning and Griffiths were not taken on, both returning to play for Swansea Town from where Griffiths became an international, so the Major's eye was not without flaw. That left John on his own in Yorkshire, but his manager showed that beneath the stern disciplinarian there was an astute and sensitive man-manager. Leeds were due to play Swansea shortly after John joined and Buckley took him down with the team. "After that I didn't feel so homesick," John remembers.

He was also helped to settle by the arrival of two more lads from Wales, Eylenn Jones and John Reynolds, a talented fullback, who had his career cut short by injury. Reynolds stayed on the groundstaff and eventually became head groundsman at Elland Road and then at the Thorp Arch training complex.

Reynolds recalls the trio used to journey back home to Wales together when they got the chance: "We travelled from Leeds Central Station which doesn't exist any more. They used to stop the night train to gather the mail and it would take about eight hours to get to Swansea. We'd toss a coin to see who would sleep on the seats and who would have to go up on the luggage rack."

The next few months brought big changes to John Charles's life. The skinny youngster was filling out and after a dozen or so games at right back, the Major switched him to centre-half for a Yorkshire League match against Barnsley.

"By this time I had grown and learned a lot. I was over six feet tall and I tipped the scales at thirteen stone - quite a change from the stripling of a boy they knew at Swansea. I could use both feet equally well, and I had learned much about the art of tackling and positional play. That game against Barnsley was the turning point in my career.

YORKSHIRE POST

MORNING EDITION   THE PRIDE OF YORKSHIRE   23RD MARCH 1951

Franklin plays well but Charles scores twice

After a season and a half impressing everyone with his commanding play at centre-half, John was switched to centre forward to boost United's ailing attack. After drawing a blank in a 4-1 defeat at Manchester City, John was on target as Leeds beat Hull City 3-0 on 23 March 1951, despite being marked by England defender Neil Franklin

Leeds United	**3**
Hull City	**0**

by RICHARD ULYATT

Interest was divided at Elland Road yesterday between the form of John Charles, Welsh international centre half now playing as Leeds United's centre forward, Neil Franklin's clash with him, and the referee's determination to finish the match despite a heavy ground which eventually became covered in snow.

Charles scored twice and thereby justified United's experiment. Franklin played delightful football, and but for him United might have won by six or seven goals, and the referee beat the snow.

All the players, the officials and that part of the 27,000 crowd which had to stand in the open, were heroes to stick it out. The crowd's part was the easiest for it was a hard, entertaining match, surprisingly full of good fotball on a day when the ball squirted in the mud, stopped in the snow, became as heavy as lead and performed unpredictable antics.

Burbanks hurt

United's forwards missed more chances than they took, but they deserve praise for having created those chances against Hull's best department, the half-back line, and while the inside forwards, Stevenson and Iggleden, worked like teriers all through the match, Peter Harrison, the outside right, was the next best forward to Charles.

He might not have been but for an injury early in the second half to Eddie Burbanks, which caused the Hull outside left to leave the field for strapping and then to retire before the end of the game. Burbanks had been the best Hull forward until that happened and as United were then only one goal up, it may have had a bearing on the result.

The rest of the Hull line, in which Smith took the place of Carter, was seldom in the game, except for Revie's help in defence and an occasional challenge by Ackerman. The defence had to bear the brunt of the work, and while Peter Harrison found a way round Varney, Hassall played nearly as well as usual in opposition to Williams.

Franklin's work

Franklin confirmed previous impressions that he is rapidly settling down. He had to cover all parts of his half of the field and he did it well. He was not once at fault when Charles scored or again when the young Welshman had a shot blocked on the line by Hassall. Charles got his goals by moving about the field; here was no orthodox down-the-middle centre-forward but a man with a football brain, able to sense the right position to take up.

Charles is not yet as good a centre forward as he is a centre half back; all his footballing life he has had the ball coming to him, now it is rolling with him and needs a different technique, but when he has mastered that he may be very good indeed. Both his goals were well taken; so, too, was Stevenson's.

Major Frank
Buckley

"I don't care how good a player is, if he can only kick with one foot, he's only half a footballer." - Major Frank Buckley

Not only did I play well enough to please all who saw the match, but I discovered that I enjoyed playing at centre-half more than wing-half or full-back. Centre-half, I felt, was my natural position."

The Major was clearly impressed. Within a few weeks, just before John's 17th birthday and signing professional, he was promoted to the reserves to play at Preston North End. Once again he produced a display that ensured he never lost his place in the team. But the meteoric rise still had one more stage to go before the end of the season.

TEENAGE SENSATION

Leeds United arranged to play a friendly against Queen of the South on Easter Tuesday, 19 April, 1949. The 'Doonhammers' were in the Scottish top flight in those days, but, more importantly from the crowd's point of view, they included centre-forward Billy Houliston who was fresh from Scotland's 3-1 triumph at Wembley where he had tormented England's finest, Neil Franklin.

Leeds' veteran first-choice centre-half, Tom Holley, had an ankle injury, so Frank Buckley decided this was the ideal opportunity to blood the promising Welsh teenager. Dick Ulyatt, of the Yorkshire Post, had been watching the youngster emerge and was delighted to report the next day: "I saw another most promising centre-half, Leeds United's 17-year-old John Charles, play his first senior match - an inter-club fixture against the Dumfries team, Queen of the South, which was drawn 0-0.

"Lacking the bite of a league fixture, the pace was not so fast as usual for many of the players. Charles was not one of these, for his opponent was William Houliston, whose refreshing vigour is welcomed by everyone except goalkeepers and centre half-backs. Young Charles came through the

ordeal no worse than the England players at Wembley a week ago, and from his cool assurance, his tactical skill and sturdy build, it seemed evident that United's manager, Major Buckley, had found a player of great promise."

According to Holley, Houliston told him afterwards that Charles was "the best centre-half I have ever met" and Major Buckley was clearly delighted because he picked John to make his league debut at Blackburn Rovers the following Saturday. The Leeds team that day was: Searson, Bannister, Milburn, McCabe, Charles, Burden, Cochrane, McMorran, Browning, Iggleden, Rudd.

John was again the outstanding player in an otherwise forgettable goalless draw and he kept his place for the final two matches of the season - a home debut, another goalless draw against Cardiff, and a 2-0 defeat at Queens Park Rangers. Injuries apart, he was never out of the Leeds side again until he left for Juventus.

Leeds finished 15th in the Second Division that season and started the new campaign poorly, picking up only six points (two for a win then) in their first eleven matches. But as the clock ticked towards a new decade, Buckley's influence started to take effect.

YORKSHIRE POST

MORNING EDITION   THE PRIDE OF YORKSHIRE   29TH NOVEMBER 1952

After experimenting with John as centre forward Major Buckley returned him to the centre of defence for all but three games in the following season. But, after an indifferent start to the 1952-53 campaign, the switch to the number nine shirt was again inevitable. The result was instant and following a 3-2 win against Brentford at Elland Road on 29 November 1952, Dick Ulyatt waxed lyrical about the young Welshman's performance.

John Charles beats Leeds United goal-scoring record

Leeds United	**3**
Brentford	**2**

by RICHARD ULYATT

For four years Major Frank Buckley has been extolling the merits of John Charles. He said, long before Charles turned out for Leeds United in his first Yorkshire League game and far in advance of the time the Welsh Soccer selectors made him, then 18 years old, their international centre half-back: "Here we have the most brilliant Association footballer in the game today and one of the outstanding in my 50 years in football." Major Buckley brought that up to date last night when he said to me:

The 'Gentle Giant' never shirked a tackle

"Charles is the best in the world. I'm very proud of him."

Playing centre-forward for United against Brentford on Saturday, Charles justified all this praise to the hilt. He did more: he proved to be a match-winner, which a centre half back never can be in these days of "stopper" football. He scored a hat-trick - his second in November, for on the first day of the month he scored three times against Hull City - he made his total of goals into 11 in League football and 13 in all matches since taking over the position in a West Riding Cup final against Halifax Town on October 8.

Passes Keetley's total

In addition he broke a club record in Football League matches, for he has now scored the club's last ten goals, thus passing Keetley's figure of seven in sequence in season 1929-30.

It must now be arguable that he is a better centre-forward than a centre half - to which position he is not likely to return as long as Jim McCabe plays well for United. There are people who say that he is too big, too clumsy, and does not fight enough for the ball. There were arguments last season about Derek Dooley, who went on scoring goals and got 46 in 30 games for Sheffield Wednesday.

Here, in parentheses, it may be noted that Major Buckley was among many managers who said: "I wish I had Dooley." Perhaps all the time he had a better Dooley - Charles, who is a more accomplished footballer.

The presence of Jim McCabe at the back enabled Charles to be pushed up front

His three goals were spectacular and therefore the purists may say that neither he nor anyone else will again score similar ones. For the second he had to turn on the icy ground, go back a yard, halt, control the ball and shoot while flurried defenders were dashing up. To score the third he had to round a bustling centre half, beat another man, take the ball from nearly half-way to the goal posts, tantalise a goalkeeper into coming out and then slip the ball into the goal.

He may not score similar goals but what convinced me above all else that his place is in the forward line was the way he dribbled on one occasion with mincing little steps in a wide arc and swerved past two men before passing the ball, which was then deflected for a corner. That was real art, the work of an accomplished footballer with the ball under control all the time, who is at his best in the open and who has been hitherto confined by the restrictions imposed on centre half-backs.

All this was on an icy surface, on which studs would not grip.

One-man win

I hesitate to use the phrase a "one-man win" but this was the nearest I have seen to it for a long time, even allowing for the terrier-like tackling of Nightingale, Kerfoot and Burden and three thrilling shots Burden made and the two goals Scott stopped, one by diving and the other by leaping and catching a ball which seemed to be going away from him.

Without Charles I doubt if United would have won for Brentford, once they had recovered from the shock of having a goal disallowed and the lead wrested from them after Dare had opened the scoring, played with determination above the ordinary and were not above using all their weight whenever possible.

By comparison with Charles, Lawton, the copy-book centre-forward for nearly a generation, was not in the picture. Perhaps that was due to the unobtrusive McCabe. Brentford's best forward was their outside-left Legerton, who from the inside right position caused Scott to make his spectacular dive and who made the score 2-2 with a header after D'Arcy had passed instead of shooting.

Attendance: 16,000

Leeds moved into the 1950s with higher confidence and improved form, finishing the season in fifth place. John Charles played in every match and scored the first of his goals for the club, slamming home a penalty in a 2-1 win at Plymouth. The resurgence, which started with three victories in a row in October, included a run of six straight league wins from New Year's Eve in Swansea to a home success over Luton in mid February. With an FA Cup run under way, the crowds were starting to flock to Elland Road - over 50,476 to see a 3-0 win over Spurs, who went on to take the championship and then won the First Division at their first attempt, 51,488 for a tense fourth round FA Cup tie against Nat Lofthouse's First Division Bolton, and 53,099 for the 3-1 fifth round victory over Cardiff.

That booked Leeds a quarter-final tie against Arsenal at Highbury, a match John still recalls as one of the most memorable of his career.

The Arsenal team was a galaxy of stars from goalkeeper George Swindin to left-winger and Test cricketer, Denis Compton. How could Second Division Leeds stand a chance against full-backs like England's Laurie Scott and Wales's Wally Barnes, and an international half-back line of Alex Forbes, Leslie Compton and Joe Mercer, that season's Footballer of the Year? Then there was the forward line alongside Brylcreem Boy Denis: Freddie Cox, Jimmy Logie, Don Roper, and Reg Lewis. This was mission impossible and London experts saw the game as a mere formality for the mighty Gunners.

It wasn't seen that way in Yorkshire. There had never been a demand for tickets like it at Elland Road. Around 150 coaches set off for London and extra ticket collectors had to be put on at Highbury underground station to cope, as the first of the 62,573 fans started to queue early on the morning of 4 March.

With a cash bonanza guaranteed, the Leeds United directors allowed the team to travel down by train the day before and stay in a London hotel, a rare treat. If the players were nervous they certainly didn't show it and they turned in a stirring performance, especially at the back where experienced full-backs Jimmy Dunn and Jack Milburn snuffed out

Leeds keeper Harry Searson tidies up as Denis Compton advances during the epic FA Cup tie at Arsenal

Arsenal's Captain Marvel, Joe Mercer

the danger from the wings and John Charles kept Roper quiet.

Even when Lewis turned in Forbes's left-wing cross in the 52nd minute, Leeds didn't give up. Swindin got a knee in the way of Frank Dudley's goal-bound shot, and Ray Iggleden hit the bar in the dying seconds.

Arsenal went on to lift the Cup, beating Liverpool 2-0 in the final, while it could be argued that the effort put in by Leeds that day cost them a spot in Division One. They won only two of their next nine matches, most importantly crashing 5-2 in front of over 50,000 people at Sheffield Wednesday who went on to clinch the second promotion place.

The next season followed a familiar pattern. After an opening day win over Doncaster Rovers, Leeds won only two of their next twelve before recovering somewhat to finish fifth again. And there was little in the way of FA Cup glory to compensate - thrashed 4-0 by Manchester United in the fourth round.

Yet with their season as good as over, United's match at Manchester City on 24 March took on a

special significance because Major Buckley played another hunch, moving John Charles to centre forward. It was not an instant success, dismissed in a mere paragraph in the newspapers the following Monday: "United's centre-forward John Charles tried very hard and well, looked the all-round and wholehearted footballer he is, but was comparatively innocuous in front of goal. His distribution in approach was, on the other hand, excellent."

Two days later, the new number nine earned rave reviews with two goals in a 3-0 home win over Hull City, and after returning to centre-half for the visit to Notts County, rounded off the season with the only goal to beat Grimsby.

From 1950-52 John was doing his National Service with the 12th Royal Lancers based at Carlisle, where he tried his hand at boxing, a career cut short by the Amateur Boxing Association because he was a professional sportsman. The army allowed him to turn out all the time for Leeds but also saw to it that he played for them, and in 1952 Trooper WJ Charles skippered his side to victory in the Army Cup. It was also during his army service that he had operations to repair cartilages in both knees.

Surgery meant John missed a large chunk of the 1951-52 season. When he returned in December, and for most of the next season and a half, Buckley decided he needed him more at the back. John pulled on the nine shirt for only the last three games that season, without scoring, and was

Trooper John Charles receives the Army Cup

back as the pillar of the defence for the first dozen games of the next campaign.

But the thought of such talent and heading power at the point of his attack was an itch Buckley couldn't ignore and he used the West Riding Cup match against Halifax to take another look. Switching Irish wing-half Jim McCabe to centre-half, he pushed John forward once more and was immediately rewarded with both goals in a 2-1 win. That settled it for the Major. For the rest of the season John was up front, and the goals started to flow. In the next seven games he failed to score only once, finding the net 13 times, including hat-tricks against Hull City and Brentford. Ronald Crowther, of the Yorkshire Evening News, described the first of those as: "one of the finest displays of devastating markmanship that I have ever seen from an Elland Road leader in post-war times." The three on a frost-bound pitch against Brentford meant John had scored Leeds' last ten goals, breaking a record of seven in sequence by Charlie Keetley 22 years before. It also saw the young Welshman described as "a great centre-forward" by no lesser judge than Brentford's striker Tommy Lawton.

The third goal, in the closing minute, remains firmly in John's memory as one of the best he ever scored. He described it in detail in King of Soccer: "I got the ball in my own half and set off for goal. Three times I was tackled and three times I managed to slip away. Then I had only the goalkeeper to beat, but I managed to swerve past him. Unfortunately I was going at top speed and the foothold was treacherous, so there was still a chance that I would fluff an open goal - especially as I saw one of the Brentford defenders coming across the goal-line to block my view of the net. However, all went well, the ball went into the net and we won 3-2."

Another hat-trick flew in to clinch a 4-0 win over Rotherham, and John finished his 30-match spell as a striker with an incredible 29 goals.

The other significant moment that season came in the final match, a 1-1 home draw against Doncaster Rovers, when Jack Charlton, the gangling Geordie nephew of Jim Milburn, who had moved to Bradford, made his debut a month before his 18th birthday.

It would be a couple more years before he would command a regular place in the team but there was no turning back for John, and while Nat Lofthouse expressed relief that he no longer had to tangle with him, centre-halves up and down the country started to have nightmares.

There was a big change, however, at Leeds United because Major Buckley decided it was time to move on again, this time to Walsall.

Just as Hull City had when Buckley left Boothferry Park, United turned to Raich Carter to take over as manager.

Carter had been one of the finest inside-forwards to play the game, enjoying memorable spells with Sunderland and Derby County, winning a league championship medal, becoming the youngest captain of a First Division side, and the only man to win FA Cup medals either side of World War II. The war meant he won only 13 full caps for England but he and Stanley Matthews formed a magnificent partnership in a series of war-time internationals.

As player-manager at Hull he led them to promotion from the Third Division North before retiring to run a sweet shop. He was persuaded to take up the managerial reins once more at Cork Athletic, leading them to the FA of Ireland Cup final in 1953. Now he was given the task of building on the Major's work and getting Leeds into the First Division.

Charles performed better than his new boss could have dreamed, starting with four goals against Notts County and three against Rotherham in the space of four days on the way to 44 in all competitions, 42 in the league. But Leeds finished only tenth and Carter was aware that it was increasingly important to get out of the Second Division or Leeds would be in grave danger of losing their prime asset.

Much as today, rumours of big-money bids for the best players were meat and drink to those who had to fill the the sports pages of newspapers, and John earned more than his share of column inches. Chairman Sam Bolton was forever denying a new bid or emphasising that Leeds were not willing to part at any price - even though for a club with few resources, Cardiff City's £40,000 bid in 1953 must have been a great temptation.

With only one victory in their first six matches of the 1954-55 season, and finding himself switched back to centre-half, John decided to bring things to a head and put in a transfer request. The directors were worried and called a meeting on the evening of 29 September to discuss the letter.

In the Yorkshire Post that morning, Eric Stanger described the decision they had to make as "the most difficult in the 35 years of the club's history." In a long article he gave a clear picture of the situation professional footballers in England faced at that time: "According to Football League law, John Charles cannot substantially earn any more money with Arsenal, Cardiff City or (if they will forgive me for using them as an illustration) Halifax Town than with Leeds United. He can be paid no more than the legal maximum of £15 a week during the playing season, plus a bonus of £2 for a win and £1 for a draw. A player of his standing can command the customary maximum Football League benefit of £750 every five years, no matter where he plays.

"Why then does Charles seek a move? As he would be the first to admit, he has been as well treated at Elland Road as anywhere. He wants to play in First Division football. Can one blame him for that? His abilities are extraordinary and one can scarcely quarrel with any artist for wishing to exploit his talents in the best medium. In Charles's case, he feels it lies in top-class football with a better team than Leeds United."

Stanger admitted he was glad he didn't have to make the decision but came down in favour of taking the cash and using it to strengthen the team in several positions.

That night Leeds played a friendly, attended by Cardiff City manager Cyril Spiers who was willing to increase his previous offer to £50,000

given the slightest encouragement. Arsenal were also watching the situation and at Chelsea, manager Ted Drake was ready with a bid.

The next morning, the Yorkshire Post carried the news that Leeds had turned down the request. John was quoted: "I'm still anxious to play First Division football but what can I do? I was called into the meeting and told that the club would not let me go. I was not really surprised."

When you consider the tantrums and pet-lips from some of today's footballers when the club decides they will not have their way, John's dignified response and, more impressively, his continued contribution on the field, spoke volumes for his character. Playing at centre-half, he drove on the team and with an undefeated run of eight games at the end of the campaign, including a 4-0 thrashing of promoted Luton Town, they lifted themselves to fourth, one point behind the three clubs above them.

Leeds were again a force to be reckoned with in the Second Division and the following season John would lead them to even greater heights. But he was also involved in spearheading arguably the greatest era of Welsh international football.

I Remember John

BARRY FOSTER has written about soccer for over forty years, twenty-seven of them as the Yorkshire Post's chief football reporter, covering not only Yorkshire clubs - including Don Revie's great Leeds team - but England and World Cups. He wrote this tribute especially for this book:

"I was skimming through an article by Leeds United's chairman Peter Ridsdale about his love affair with the club, and it was suddenly brought home to me what a huge influence John Charles played on my life-time association with football.

Peter Ridsdale talked about going to his first game at Elland Road as a seven year old in 1959 ('If I remember rightly the game was against Grimsby Town') and the journey which has taken him from the boys' pen on the old Kop at Leeds to the chairman's seat.

His tale brought the memories flooding back: suddenly I could see the quartered blue and old gold jerseys again, the bone-shuddering tackles of big Tom Holley, who was later to become a sports writer and friend, and busy Albert Wakefield leading the attack. As a nine year old, I was smitten with the professional game from that first match when Leeds ran in five goals against Plymouth Argyle in early September, twelve years before the chairman's debut.

I recall that John Short, an elegant inside-left who scored that day, was my first hero; remember that soon my dad and big brother (both Percys, a forgotten name these days) would take me on the 54 bus from Rodley to the bottom of Armley Road. We would get off at the White Horse pub and walk through the back-to-back streets off Gelderd Road before cutting across what was then largely unused open fields, jumping Low Beck, and arriving an hour before the kick off so I could get a good vantage point on one of the concrete blocks which held the goal stanchions in place.

Barry Foster

After the match the crowds would surge down the Kop bank and race across Low Fields Road to jump on any one of the line of moving trams which seemed to clear the masses like magic, back to the city centre.

But most of all, I remember Big John. He got into the Leeds side towards the end of the following season as a teenager and by then I was a regular at Elland Road. Over the eight years of his first spell with Leeds, I grew up with him, dazzled by his growing dominance and becoming surer by the week that I had to be involved in some way with soccer.

Every week Charles seemed to get better, bigger, stronger. Soon he was a giant in all aspects of the game.

I can still feel the wall reverberating as I stood at the front of the same boys' pen Peter Ridsdale would occupy, when, for once, Charles missed the target with a thuderbolt of a shot which smacked into the concrete as I ducked out of the way.

I can still see him rise to meet a cross from the diminutive Harold Williams. Somehow he managed to hang in the air and find a moment to glance at the corner of the net before powering a twelve-yard header home with the force usually associated with a ball struck by a boot.

For such a big man he had a delicate touch, too, on the ball and, times without number in his centre half days, he would advance from deep in the Leeds half with the ball glued to his feet, drifting by one opponent, tricking the next, flowing past the next before sliding the ball down the inside-right slot to Ray Iggleden, or to Frank Dudley on the left.

Throughout those years one writer, perhaps more passionately than any other, captured in word pictures Big John's progress from signing as a 16 year old, to his international debut days after his 18th birthday, onwards through the enormous influence he had on the Leeds team of the 1950s and on to his high-profile move to Italy where, with Juventus, he became an icon all over again.

Ron Crowther was the Sports Editor of the Yorkshire Evening News and the most fluent sports writer I have ever known. He played a massive role in bringing Charles into the limelight, rattling out words by the thousand on the Welsh genius. It was my good fortune in my early days in the newspaper business to be taken under his wing.

One of the first assignments he gave me was to go and see Big John's wife at a Morley nursing home, hours after one of his infants had arrived.

I remember Ron and his deputy Jack Gillings telling the story about passing Elland Road late one night after they had been to a match, when they heard what appeared to be rifle shots coming from the back of the west stand.

Bang, thump, crash, wallop. It sounded as though someone was intent on knocking a hole in the side of the ageing building. Elland Road was

With so little film footage of the great man in action, we have to rely largely on memories and words. But it was true that he was equally at home at either centre-half or centre forward, and when he blazed a trail to the First Division in 1956 for Leeds, it seemed as though the weekend was not complete if it had not included a goal or several from the King.

It was hard to take when he finally went to Italy. When the news broke that Juventus wanted Charles, Ron Crowther, as you might expect, was always in the forefront of the media action, and we all spent a lot of time chasing leads in what was not only a new departure for a British footballer, but something unique for the British Press to handle.

By the time he returned to Leeds five years later I was covering matches and remember going to the game at Huddersfield Town in September

"Every week Charles seemed to get better, bigger, stronger. Soon he was a giant in all aspects of the game."

not like it is today...no-one much was about to investigate. So they stopped the car and tentatively worked their way towards the noise. There, in the dark, smacking the ball with great power at the wall of the stand, was the young giant.

Charles was tuning up for the following Saturday on his own, building up the power to produce a shot that was like a cannon ball when he got the goal in his sights.

He hit one so hard one Saturday at Elland Road that when the ball struck the visitors' left hand goalpost, it rebounded into Leeds half of the field. I thought maybe that was a flight of fancy, that it was something I thought I had seen, but before sitting down to write this piece, I checked it out with Jack Gillings and he, too, knew all about that powerful shot.

One of my greatest disappointments before joining the News was being unable, because of the scarcity of tickets and the cost of going to London, to go to Leeds's FA Cup sixth round trip to Arsenal in 1950. I gobbled up every spoken word of the radio commentary, and watched the newsreels the following week which showed how well Leeds had done to take Arsenal to the brink, and how Charles had played such a mighty role.

1962 with stars in my eyes. But some of the magic had gone even though Big John still had a powerful presence.

It was not long before he was off again to Italy and, while the reign of Leeds as a team was just about to begin, the reign of King John was over.

I remember feeling a great sadness for the new Leeds followers of the time who could not understand what all the fuss had been about. They had not been privileged to see Charles in all his majesty but there is no doubt in my mind that in his prime he was the most complete footballer I have ever seen.

It was inconceivable that he could be beaten by an attacker when he was at centre half, inconceivable that he could be held by a defender when he played at centre forward. I might have been at my most impressionable age as far as football was concerned when Charles was King, but, Pele apart, there is hardly a top player I have not seen 'live' over the last fifty years, so I have plenty of comparisons upon which to draw.

And I would have no hesitation about the first name I would put down on any list if I had to pick the best team of all time."

YORKSHIRE POST

MORNING EDITION   THE PRIDE OF YORKSHIRE   19TH AUGUST 1953

After 29 goals in 30 games up front, it was no surprise when John started the new campaign as centre forward. And he was immediately back in the old routine, scoring four times in the opening match on 19 August 1953.

Only Charles could have scored these

Leeds United	**6**
Notts County	**0**

by RICHARD ULYATT

Even Mr Hilton Crowther, longest serving Leeds United director, could not remember the club getting off to such a magnificent start as this; my records show that they have not since the war scored such an emphatic win. Raich Carter, the new manager, no doubt

Raich Carter

was happy about it, but he controlled his enthusiasm and regretted only that the crowd was no more than 18,000. No doubt he will be better pleased with Saturdays's gate when Leeds are at home to Rotherham.

Apart from the rain, Elland Road was just as John Charles and United like it - slightly holding with the ball kept down by the wet and the going on the slow side. Of course they used it and in Charles they had the man fully to exploit any situation in which he found the opposing defence slightly slow to meet him and hesitant to cover up.

Burbanks starts well

It was not by any means a one-man win. The two wing half-backs played grand supporting football. Williams, considering his long lay-off, had a most satisfactory game, scored once and deserved two goals. Burbanks on the other wing, helped in several of the goals, did all that was expected of him and, above all, was nine times out of ten in position - always a potential source of danger to the opposition.

But when due credit is given to the support of the Leeds players, and allowance is made for the untidy Notts defence and their reluctance to drive home promising attacks in which footcraft was the equal, often the superior of United's, this was Charles's match.

No average centre-forward would have scored the first goal when he threw himself past Leuty to head Burden's speculative centre from the wing past a startled goalkeeper; few players would be able to conrol the ball so well as he and, nine inches from the dead-ball line, screw it past County's goalkeeper, who grasped it but was unable to stop it entering the net for the second goal.

His third was neatly headed from Burbanks's centre, his fourth (United's fifth) was perhaps the only one a centre-forward of average ability would have scored. Burbanks's corner kick grazed Charles's head before Williams shot the fourth goal. Nightingale rounded off the scoring, starting and finishing a movement in which his final pass ought to have gone to Charles instead of Williams. In addition these ebullient United forwards had the ball in the net nine times.

PRINCE OF WALES

John Charles's introduction to international football was a flop.

He had played only 39 league games when he fulfilled Major Buckley's confident prediction that he would claim the centre-half shirt for Wales. He was 18 years 71 days old when he ran out against Ireland, the youngest Welshman to win a cap until Ryan Giggs took over that distinction in 1992.

It was not only the Welsh selectors who felt John was good and ready. Dick Ulyatt, of the Yorkshire Post, was full of anticipation as he wrote: "I am going to Wrexham just to see how United's 18-year-old star shines in his new firmament, and I have no doubt that he will illuminate the scene just as steadily and strongly as he does a league match."

But the thought of pulling on the red shirt and lining up alongside boyhood heroes like Roy Paul, Trevor Ford, Ronnie Burgess, Alf Sherwood and Wally Barnes made the youngster freeze. Canny old Aston Villa centre-forward Dave Walsh gave the young upstart a tough afternoon, but most of John's problems were self inflicted.

He recalled: "It semed like only yesterday that I was a starry eyed youngster on the ground staff at Swansea, proud to look after the boots of Roy Paul and Trevor Ford. Now I was playing with them in the same Welsh international team. It was incredible.

"But I had reckoned without the footballer's biggest enemy - nerves. My sturdy legs turned to jelly. My stomach was devoured by a battalion of butterflies. My vision and judgement were clouded by worry - worry that I would make a mistake."

The game ended goalless but the press were quick to point out Charles's shortcomings. Even the faithful Ulyatt came close to writing a critical report: "Young John confessed to me before the start of the match that he was nervous. His play for the whole of the first 45 minutes provided confirmation. By normal standards, he played quite well but Charles has set an unusually high level of achievement and on this occasion he did not reach it."

John returned to Leeds in despair but the Major quickly restored his self confidence and assured him he would have the chance to put things right one day. It took a year before that opportunity came, against Switzerland in one of the matches arranged to celebrate the Festival of Britain.

Wales took a 3-0 lead before John experienced what he described as "the worst 20 minutes of my life." The Swiss centre-forward and skipper, Bickel, started to roam, causing the youngster problems he'd not encountered before, and with ten minutes still to go the score was back to 3-2. "From that moment we had to hang on grimly, and we did!" John said.

The selectors again decided they had made a mistake and it was 1953 before they turned to Charles again. By now he was a prolific centre-forward for Leeds, and Wales had just been trounced 5-2 by England. Ray Daniel was centre-half, Trevor Ford at centre-forward, so for the game against Ireland in Belfast space was made for John at inside

right in a forward line made in Swansea: Medwin, Charles, Ford, Allchurch, Griffiths.

Danny Blanchflower marshalled the Irish brilliantly and Wales found themselves a goal down after twenty minutes, but ten minutes later Harry Griffiths - the lad who had joined John on trial at Leeds but been rejected - hooked the ball into the box and John slammed it home with his left foot.

Terry Medwin produced the cross for John to head Wales in front and, sacrificing the chance to

I Remember John

Cliff Morgan

CLIFF MORGAN and John Charles are Welsh Gods. While John was inspiring a generation of footballers, Cliff was mesmerising the rugby world. Arguably one of the finest rugby players ever, Cliff went on to a career in broadcasting where he showed the same wonderful flair. Where once it had been with a dummy, a sidestep, or a change of pace, now it was that wonderful rich voice, the perfectly chosen phrase and a vision of what sport could be that captured people's hearts and imagination. He said of John:

"We were taught in the Rhonda Valley that you looked up to people. You looked up to politicians, great Prime Ministers and great figures. John Charles was someone you looked up to and you said 'That is something different'.

People ask would sportsmen like John, Denis Compton and the stars of those days, be as good today? Of course, it's impossible to judge because the games have changed so much. But for me John Charles would have been a star in any generation.

He was a different class. He was never sent off the field. He had good elbows, mind. But he was always the perfect sportsman.

He had all the principles that I admire in sport and he stands apart as someone who had a magnetic influence on a nation.

"If he was playing, there were always thousands extra on the gate. People wanted to see him play."

When he went to Italy, what they liked about him was his Welshness, his honesty, sincerity and his ability.

He never acted like a big star. He was part of the team. And when people used to go up and stand outside his flat, he used to invite them in and give them a drink. I love that.

We were contemporaries. I'd meet him in the early 1950s and on through into the 60s. In those days you met each other - rugby players, cricketers, football players.

At that time Welsh sport was in great, great heart with wonderful players at both football and rugby.

The war had been on. Suddenly it was over and there was sport. People didn't have money, they didn't have cars, there was nothing else to do. But you could afford to go to a football match or a rugby match in those days. Now if you're a kid, you can't.

Great sportsmen always stand out. You didn't have to see Gary Sobers batting to know he was special. You just had to see him walk to the wicket and take guard. And it was the same with John Charles. If he was playing, there were always thousands extra on the gate. People wanted to see him play.

And John loved to play for them. He loved the fact that he was gifted by God with a talent to play football."

score a hat-trick, John set up Trevor Ford for the third. At last he had produced the form for his country that he showed week-in, week-out for his club, and there was no turning back.

That October, Wales took on England at Cardiff, outplayed them and lost 4-1 after an injury to Alf Sherwood saw them reduced to ten men for about 17 minutes during which time England scored all four of their goals. But 'An Old International', writing in the Manchester Guardian, made sure his readers realised how superior Wales had been up to then: "Meanwhile, how faired it with the Englishry? By the end of a quarter of an hour Wright was drawing in great gulps of breath as might a vagrant trombonist trying to play the Hallelujah Chorus and escape from the police at the same time. Dickinson was frankly puzzled. Why were all his choicest passes coming back so quickly? Where had Wilshaw and Quixall hidden themselves? As for Johnston, poor chap, he might as well have been at Palomart Observatory star gazing." As usual, Ulyatt was there for the Yorkshire Post and reported: "Charles was magnificent. The 61,000 Welshmen present talked about his football for hours after the match, the newspaper men ran out of superlatives. One, whose comments I quoted in my report of the match last Monday, declared Charles to be as great as, perhaps greater than, the fabulous Dixie Dean."

The luck of the English struck again in November 1954 when John made his Wembley debut. Again the Welsh were well on top until injuries to Ray Daniel and Derek Sullivan allowed England to come back and win a rainswept enounter 3-2. Roy Bentley grabbed the headlines with a hat-trick but for Ulyatt, Charles's second goal for Wales was the highlight: "His second goal, which was the middle one of three scored in six minutes during the second half, was an entirely different affair (from the tapped-in first), the ball going squarely to him from the touchline and John taking it along the penalty area line with such deliberation that I thought he would lose it. Eventually he transferred it to his right foot and then cracked in a shot along the ground which had Wood beaten before he could move."

Wales finally got justice in October 1955 when they beat England 2-1 at Cardiff, their first win over their arch rivals for 17 years. Derek Tapscott and Cliff Jones put Wales in front only for England to pull one back, John Charles heading into his own net! "Even that couldn't spoil the day," John said. "It is a day that will live long in the memory of every Welshman who saw the match or played in it."

Wales's greatest achievement came in 1958 when they reached the quarter-finals of the World Cup in Sweden, and John nearly missed it.

For once fate favoured the boys in red. They failed to qualify through their group but were given a second chance because Arab teams refused to play Israel. FIFA ruled that one of the 16 runners-up would play against Israel to decide who would go to Sweden, and Wales came out of the draw. They won each game of the two-legged play-off 2-0 and were bound for the World Cup finals as representatives of the Asia-Africa section. For the only time, all four home countries qualified for the finals.

Wales were managed by the charismatic Jimmy Murphy, who combined his international duties with those of assistant to Matt Busby at Manchester United. Murphy was renowned as a motivator and described by John as "a great character. His team talks were legendary and not very politically correct - I remember when we played Germany he said `These are the people who bombed your families in the war, go out and get your revenge!' He was a terrific fella."

Having guided Wales, albeit fortunately, to the finals, all Murphy's attention was focused on Old Trafford where he had to rebuild the side in Busby's absence after the Munich air crash. It was an eighteen-hour a day job, with even his snatched sleep haunted by those who had died or were still injured. Murphy took players from all over to patch up a side which reached the FA Cup final, only to be defeated by Bolton Wanderers, and it's interesting to speculate that John Charles might well have switched to Manchester United had he not just moved to Juventus.

There is little doubt that his preoccupation with the club affected Murphy's World Cup preparations and he received little help from the Wales selectors.

YORKSHIRE POST

MORNING EDITION THE PRIDE OF YORKSHIRE 10TH OCTOBER 1953

After a couple of poor games at the start of his international career, John soon became one of the stalwarts of the Wales side. His performances for his country were as mighty as those for his club, even as here on 10 October 1953, in defeat. What is particularly entertaining about this piece is how much Dicky Ulyatt enjoyed the success of the lad he'd been praising from the start of his career.

Wales   **1**
England   **4**

by RICHARD ULYATT

Another chance for lucky FA team

The brilliance of John Charles

England's Association Football selectors have to tackle a pretty problem this week: to sack or not sack a winning team. I come down heavily on the side of the leave-them-alone school, but only because I am firmly convinced that every team must be given another chance of confirming praise or being double damned.

On the evidence of Saturday's international championship match at Cardiff only Merrick (goalkeeper), Dickinson (left half-back) and perhaps Lofthouse (centre-forward) would be retained by the sack-em critics who might with even more justification demand the heads of England's selectors and team-manager for

Brothers in arms: Welsh football in the 1950s was blessed with two sets of outstanding, Swansea-born brothers - John and Mel Charles, and Len and Ivor Allchurch

*Nat Lofthouse -
on target twice for England*

their bungling selections, even though the team manager did halt the axe in mid-air by what I assume were his half-time instructions.

Best since Dean

All the Sunday newspapers I read yesterday commented that England were lucky to win. Most of them said that the result was a travesty of justice, some said this was the worst England side ever selected. All said that John Charles, the Welsh and Leeds United centre forward, was the outstanding player. One even said he must be: 'Written down as the greatest and most artistically efficient since Dean led the England attack. If it is insisted, as it may be, that Lawton was as good as Dean, then Charles must be accounted better than either.'

I quote that because for four years I have been saying much the same of this genial giant who will not be 22 until the end of December and any further praise from me may be accounted fulsome. I write it with great satisfaction because when in the spring of 1950 Charles played at centre half for Wales after I had cracked him up as the best centre half of my time, he gave such a pathetically feeble exposition that the London critics looked at me out of pitying and contemptuous eyes. This time I was able to smile and say: 'I told you so' as they gobbled up all the details I could give them of the great Charles's career and habits.

Superb Merrick

Charles was as magnificent as the few soccer enthusiasts there are in Leeds know he can be. He beat the sturdy centre-half Johnston nine times out of ten in the air and nearly as often on the ground.

A dozen times his headers or shots were either inches wide or saved by the superb Merrick. He dummied to go to the left, passed to the right and Davies pushed the ball on for Allchurch to score Wales's goal. He put two passes at the feet of Davies which ought to have been shot into the goal instead of high over it. At that stage it was unbelievable Wales would lose; if it really had been Charles's day he would have scored five or six

goals and made several others, surely it was only a question of time?

Then why did Wales lose? The short answer is: because of an injury to their left back Sherwood and the time-table of vital incidents bears that out (figures representing minutes):

22 Allchurch goal
(Burgess, Charles, Davies passes)

35 Sherwood off, concussion

44 Wilshaw headed goal, from Quixall's free kick

50 Wilshaw headed goal
(Eckersley pass, Mullen long cross)

51 Lofthouse headed goal
(Mullen pass)

51 ½ Sherwood on the field at outside left

53 Lofthouse headed goal
(Mullen pass)

Two to one

Not until half-time did England realise that the rearrangement of the Welsh team resulting from Sherwood's injury had weakened the Welsh attack from which Charles's most powerful ally, the ebullient Allchurch, was withdrawn. England were left with a surplus man in defence - Garrett, the right back - and for the whole of the second half Garrett, in addition to Johnston, gravitated on Charles whenever the ball approached England's penalty area. Thus Charles had two men to beat, one before and one after receiving the ball, and consequently Merrick had a much happier second half.

International officials were generally a joke, blazered tradesmen who manned the endless committees more because of their involvement with a local league than their understanding of professional football.

Wales was particularly badly served by well-meaning men who didn't have a clue, but swanned around the world looking important. John recalled one typical incident after Wales had been defeated 3-1 by Scotland at Hampden Park: "We were sitting in a lounge having a cup of tea after the game when one of our selectors came in and said: 'Well done, lads. You were far too strong for us today.' We laughed and said: 'But Mr Owens, we're the Welsh team.'

"On another occasion we were flying off to a match when they found there weren't enough places on the plane, so the officials all got on and made one of the players wait for a later flight."

Cliff Jones, the world-class left winger for Wales and Spurs, also recalls an occasion when an official's knowledge of his players was not quite what it might have been: "Brazil had been so impressed with our performances in the 1958 World Cup, that they invited us over for a couple of warm-up matches in 1962. We arrived back at the end of a three week tour and were on the bus taking us from the plane to the arrival lounge, when one of the selectors said to Dave Hollins: 'Where have you been?' When Dave told him, he replied: 'That's a coincidence, I've just come back from a football tour over there.' Three weeks and he still didn't recognise his own player. We used to call them the first eleven, because they always got on planes and checked into hotels first to make sure they had the best of everything. They meant well but most of them had never been out of Wales and they really didn't have much of a clue."

While everyone recognised the importance of John Charles to the team, the selectors were tardy in getting his release from Juventus for the World Cup.

Charismatic coach Jimmy Murphy was renowned for the inspirational team-talks to the Welsh squad

I Remember John

Western Mail and Echo

CLIFF JONES was one of the finest wingers of his generation, skilful, brave, lightning quick and incredibly good in the air for a man around 5ft 6in tall. He won 59 caps for Wales and became the world's most expensive winger at £35,000 in 1958 when he left Swansea Town for Spurs. At White Hart Lane he became a key member of the 1961 double winning side, won three FA Cup winners' medals, and a European Cup Winners' Cup medal when Spurs thrashed Atletico Madrid.

A member of a unique footballing family, which could boast at least one member registered with the Football League for more than 50 years from 1918, Cliff recalls his first impressions of John Charles:

"John was certainly the greatest all-round player this country ever produced. I suppose the next one to him would be Duncan Edwards but, unfortunately, we never had the chance to see him develop fully.

The first game I ever played for Wales was in 1955. We played Austria in Vienna and John was centre-half. Back then Austria were probably the best team in Europe. They beat us 2-1 but it was only John's performance that kept the score to that level. He was absolutely superb. It was the best centre-half display I have ever seen.

Twelve months later we played England at Ninian Park. John was centre-forward. We beat England and that was the best centre forward display I have ever seen.

That was the mark of the bloke. He was such a great all-round player. And he had a wonderful temperament. Nothing ever seemed to upset him.

We had a very good team in Wales in those days. John, Ivor Allchurch, with Terry Medwin and me on the wings, Mel Charles at half-back, Mel Hopkins at full-back, Jack Kelsey in goal. I look back at it and think we should have done a lot better than we did. Individually we were quite as good as any other team but collectively we couldn't quite put it together. I don't know why.

"If John had played in the quarter-final of the 1958 World Cup against Brazil, we could have beaten them"

I still think if John had played in the quarter-final of the 1958 World Cup against Brazil, we could have beaten them. People think I'm joking but I'm convinced of it.

I had my best game of the World Cup in that game, and Terry and I provided plenty of service with crosses. Colin Webster came in at centre forward. He was a good player but he was not John Charles. John would have got on the end of one of those crosses. It's a certainty. And we would have been very, very dangerous.

I look back now to the team we had at Swansea Town - I still can't think of them as Swansea City. We had a very good side and we had about eight or nine Swansea boys in the team. The crowd were fanatical about it because we were all local youngsters.

It was a good time for Welsh football. Cardiff were in the First Division in those days and I sometimes wonder what would have happened at Swansea if they had kept hold of John. We always had good games against Leeds and always did well against them."

The thing I like about John is that he has not forgotten where he came from. He's still a Swansea boy with his feet on the ground. He's a terrific character."

YORKSHIRE POST

MORNING EDITION   THE PRIDE OF YORKSHIRE   22ND OCTOBER 1955

For most of his games for Wales, John played at centre-half, and it was there that he turned in another sparkling per-formance - despite an own goal! - on a never-to-be forgotten day when his country beat arch-rivals England on 22 October 1955. It's a match John recalls as his proudest moment in a Wales shirt.

Charles & Co master elderly England

England came out of the Cardiff crucible with national football pride badly scorched and some individual reputations con-sumed, I am afraid, in the Welsh flames. It was not so much that Wales played supremely well to earn their first win over England in a full international for 17 years but that England never bore the hall-mark of a modern national side.

They might have been an FA XI got together for some missionary game - and a rather elderly one at that. There will undoubtedly be changes - sweeping changes - for the Irish match at Wembley on November 2.

Even Stanley Matthews, though not a real failure, was not the Matthews we have come to expect, spreading alarm and confusion every time in possession. For the first time he looked something like his age and one must reluctantly wonder if even his almost everlasting career is not now drawing to a close.

Tough as a cup-tie

I would be more definite on the point but for one thing. Matthews in this game, which had few of the graces one expects in an international but all the toughness and tension of a cup-tie, never got the type of pass he wants. All football knows he likes the ball straight to his feet so that he can wiggle and jiggle to get opponents on the wrong foot before the has moved so much as a yard. This

Having paid a massive fee for John, the Italians were always reluctant to let him play for his country in case he got injured. There were no FIFA rules that country comes before club in those days, and John recalls the Welsh officials seemed reluctant to face up to the might of the Agnelli family who owned Juventus: "Mr Powell, the secretary of the Wales FA, used to write to me and ask if I could get free to play."

Everyone had assumed John would be released for Sweden but Juventus were insisting that he stay behind to play in the Italian Cup. When they finally relented, the Italian FA refused permission for him to travel because they hadn't been given enough notice of his release. The red tape seemed to take an age to sort out and Wales's star striker was finally given the go ahead to join his team-mates just four days before the opening game against Hungary.

A disrupted flight meant John arrived at the airport in Stockholm at three in the morning with not a single Welsh official there to meet him. After spending over an hour trying to find out where the team was staying, John was rescued by a journalist who drove him to the hotel. In Mario Risoli's record time he mostly had to chase it 10 or 20 yards ahead, and he never liked that even in his younger days.

If there was an outstanding personality in this game it was the young master - John Charles. He had Lofthouse under his thumb; his coolness when others about him were losing their heads must have been an inspiration; his poise as he cut out high centres with his head left 60,000 Welshmen gasping with admiration. Charles today is the uncrowned monarch of Welsh football. That he should give England their goal when he headed a long cross by Byrne into this own net early in the second half would have been football's greatest irony had it cost Wales victory.

Hammer blows

But a Welsh win was always in the offing after they had snatched two goals in the 39th and 40th minutes - two hammer blows from which England never recovered, hard though they tried

to rally in the second-half. The first came when the lively Tapscott dashed through the middle to take Allchurch's through pass. Byrne, who could never get to grips with him, this time not only missed his tackle but fell in front of Wright's path. The rest was easy for Tapscott.

The Welsh were still cheering when Tapscott was off again and from his centre, Jones, the outside left, nicked in before both Ford and Williams to head a delightful goal.

Wales's football was always more direct than England's. England sought to do everything in triangular progression. Moreover, in the first-half England were bogged down in the theory of the funnel defence - that shuffling back on one's own goal before offering challenge so beloved of Continentals but foreign to English style and nature.

Second-half change

It gave Melvyn Charles and Paul, the Welsh wing halves, yards and

yards of undisputed territory in which to work the ball. Fortunately England tossed theory aside in the second half, adopted more of an 'Up Guards and at 'em' style and effectively checked Welsh monopoly of the middle of the field.

John Charles apart, Wales owed much to the untiring efforts of his brother, the skill of Paul until he was hurt and spent the last 25 minutes limping on the left wing, the cool goalkeeping of Kelsey, the direct play of their wingers, Tapscott and Jones, and the persistent harrying by Ford, in whom the flame of patriotism never burns so bright as when England are being met.

England's successes were few, their failures many. Wright was splendid and Ford got no change out of him, but of the others in defence only Hall, the right back, and Williams in goal could plead worthiness of another chance. The forwards were a sorry lot. Only Wilshaw ever looked like snatching a goal.

of Wales in the 1958 World Cup, `When Pele Broke Our Hearts', Mel Charles tells of the reaction when his brother walked into the dining room of the Grand Hotel, Soltsjobaden: "I'll never forget it," he said. "John walked in. He looked like a Greek god because he was so tall and bronzed. The selectors saw him, threw down their knives and forks, stood up and started singing `For he's a jolly good fellow, for he's a jolly good fellow.' It was like a kids' party"

The World Cup started well for John, even though his renowned patience was tested to the limits

by the Hungarian team in the opening match. They were determined to stop him by any means and kicked lumps out of him throughout the match. But, as usual, he refused to retaliate and gained his revenge by heading home the equaliser, his country's first World Cup finals goal.

After that stirring and surprise 1-1 draw against Hungary, Wales became a bit complacent and allowed unfancied Mexico to grab an 89th minute equaliser in the second match. It was described as the worst performance by Wales since the war and John never managed to get involved in the game at all.

I Remember John

HAROLD WILLIAMS once completed his early morning milk round before travelling to Leeds where he inspired Newport County to pull off an FA Cup giant-killing. Leeds manager Major Buckley was so impressed with the winger with the size five boots that he signed him for £12,000, so bringing Harold back into contact with John Charles, the lad he'd known from his earliest days in the game. They remain friends to this day.

"I've known John since he was 14 years old - over 53 years. That's a long time. He was on the groundstaff at Swansea when I was playing for Newport County.

I came out of the navy and tried to get fixed up at Swansea but they couldn't take me. They had to take players back after the war and had so many on the groundstaff they couldn't fit me in.

My mother said: 'Newport County's been here for you' and within eighteen months I was in the international team, and two years later I was transferred to Leeds United and joined up with John. And we're both still up here.

I always remember one of the trainers at Swansea, Joe Sykes. He was a good friend of mine and he used to say to me 'This boy's going to be a fantastic player.'

I used to think 'I dunno.' He was a big lad, a bit slow then, but Joe's words came true.

My personal feelings are that I have never seen a better footballer. He was an exception to every rule. Even if he had a bad game, he'd probably score two or three goals.

There's certainly never been a player as good as him at centre half. He was brilliant. But they put him at centre-forward because he was wasted at centre-half. An absolutely tremendous player."

> *"I have never seen a better footballer. He was an exception to every rule."*

For the third game, against the hosts, Murphy decided a goalless draw would do to ensure a play-off to get into the quarter finals, so he played John in midfield and then moved him back into defence alongside brother Mel. It was far from pretty but it paid off and Wales once again faced Hungary for the right to meet Brazil.

That success once more created embarrassment for the team's officials who had been so certain Wales would be beaten by Sweden, they had booked their flights home. They had to leave the team hotel, fly back to London then buy tickets back to Stockholm the next day.

John was being heavily criticised by the Swedish press who had expected him to be one of the star turns of the World Cup and things got worse for him in the play-off.

He played with four stitches in an eye wound received against Sweden, and once more found himself on the end of savage treatment by the Magyars. Wales recovered from going a goal down to win the match with a dream 25-yard goal by Ivor Allchurch and a second from Terry Medwin, but John's World Cup was over. The brutal tackling, especially one from Sipos, left him limping and unable to play in the quarter-final.

His absence made all the difference and Wales were eliminated by a toe poke by 17-year-old Pele. Cliff Jones is not alone in thinking his country might have pulled off the biggest shock in their history if their Juventus star had been playing. "Terry Medwin and I got in some decent crosses that day and I can't believe John wouldn't have got on the end of one of them," he said.

John describes missing that match as "the biggest disappointment of my career" but adds, "playing for Wales was always very special for me. I always wanted to pull on the shirt and represent my country. It was an honour."

DIVISION ONE AT LAST

Take any of today's post-Bosman footballers, transport them in a time machine back to the early 1950s and they would find themselves in an alien world, little of which they would recognise.

The maximum wage meant that a top star of that era earned in a year what a middle-range Premiership player of today sees added to his bank balance every 12 hours. Today, club car parks are filled with BMWs, Porsches and Jaguars and players roar off after a match to their luxury homes behind security gates. Fifty years ago it was usually a club house and if any of the players managed to buy a second-hand car, he was the most popular guy at the club.

Players were owned by the clubs who were not in the game to cosset footballers, and were not worried if they upset them. Jimmy Armfield, later to captain England, recalls that while at Blackpool, he spent one summer building a garage on to his club house. "I was summoned by the directors who told me that now I had a garage, my rent would go up from two pounds a week to two pounds ten shillings. When I protested that I'd done all the work myself, paid for the materials and added value to their property, they just replied that they hadn't asked me to do it."

John Charles recalls the set-up at Leeds: "Most of us lived in a club house on the estate opposite the ground. I was there with Andy McCall, Archie Gibson, Harold Williams, Bob Forrest, Jimmy Dunn and Jack Charlton. We used to walk down to the ground for training and matches."

One thing modern players would probably appreciate was the restrained and largely unobtrusive media coverage. TV showed the occasional international and the FA Cup final - Match of the Day was still ten years away - and the BBC was the only radio station with its football largely concentrated in Sports Report. Newspaper reporters mixed socially with players and cared not one jot about their love-lives, drinking or other habits - Stanley Matthews made a few bob advertising Craven A cigarettes. Apart from that, news-hungry fans had to rely on Charlie Buchan's Football Monthly, which never carried a whiff of controversy or scandal. Web sites, ClubCall, post-match phone-ins and dirt-raking were not even imagined.

For most fans, footballers came out of the tunnel just before three o'clock on Saturday, performed like Gods, and disappeared again down the tunnel at twenty to five, not to be heard of again for seven days.

YORKSHIRE POST

MORNING EDITION   THE PRIDE OF YORKSHIRE   25TH FEBRUARY 1956

After years of missing out on promotion despite John's consistent brilliance, United finally made the breakthrough in the 1955-56 season. Manager Raich Carter started John off at centre half or right wing half and then shifted him back to centre forward. But after a run of six matches with only one victory, he switched John to the inside right berth and produced an instant success against top of the table Sheffield Wednesday on 25 February 1956

Now seven clubs are rivals for Division II lead

Charles-Forrest change a great success

Leeds United   2
Sheffield Wednesday   1

by RICHARD ULYATT

If the Football League management committee had visited Elland Road, Leeds, on Saturday - not a far-fetched suggestion really, for many clubs whose matches were snowed off were represented - they might have wondered if their famous five point manifesto issued earlier in the month had been really necessary.

They would have noticed that the attendance (43,000) was twice as big as some United have had this season, they would have seen an exciting match in which the football was always interesting and sometimes clever, and they would have been encouraged by the reactions of an enthusiastic crowd.

They might have seen that spectators would flock in thousands to see a match which promised to be interesting and that it was not necessary to reshape the League.

This was, of course, a special occasion, for both clubs had their eyes on promotion, and it was linked with an exceptionally attractive Second Division programme in which six leaders were opposed. The result of this much advanced Leeds United from sixth to fifth place in the table and weakened Sheffield Wednesday's hold on the leadership. There are now six clubs within four points of them, one of whom, Liverpool, oppose Leeds United in Liverpool on Wednesday.

Promotion is a keen spur and I am sure that had the management committee been there they would have agreed that we ought to have more of it.

Both these teams would find First Division football hard going but on the evidence of their determination to get there, they would not fail for want of trying. Sheffield Wednesday were the more accomplished side because in Staniforth they had a polished full back, in McEvoy a centre half who gave the willing Charlton a lesson in calm deliberation and studied distribution, and wing half backs who scented where the danger lay and went there at full speed.

That was why John Charles was closely marked by Ralph O'Donnell, a centre-half who has been converted to wing half with considerable success. Charles was United's inside-right in this match and it is probable that he will stay in that position for a long time if this form is not just a flash in the pan.

It was because of his readiness to shoot that United looked so much more dangerous than Wednesday. At the end of the first half, United were a goal

John skippers the Leeds team of 1954-55

up and had shot at goal four times to every once by Wednesday whose only reward was a series of corner kicks.

Charles's best game

This in many ways was the best game Charles has ever played for Leeds United. At centre half we have seen his brilliance dominate the scene when United were in danger. At centre-forward we have seen him make backs and goalkeepers look foolishly simple. The trouble has been that he has not been employed all the time.

His few games at inside-right have not been a success hitherto for one reason or another, largely it seemed because he was slow to turn, like all big men.

The covering of snow cushioned the ball and gave Charles just that extra fragment of time he needed; his boisterous opponents only rarely stooped to illegal means to stop him; they played football.

Charles was the complete footballer in defence and attack. When players reach his eminence it often happens that their popularity acts as a boomerang. One hears whispers that "so-and-so is not training; he only tries when he wants to." Charles stopped the slanderous tongues before they had got loudly wagging by showing that he was fit, was trying every second and was the best footballer of an accomplished company.

Only one man in the ground has ever given a better version of inside right play and he not very often - Raich Carter, United's manager, who was sitting in the stand.

Forrest's header

Charles scored the first goal with a deliberate shot after Overfield had swung the ball across to Forrest, whose header was parried by McIntosh but not caught as it should have been. Forrest scored the vital goal in the second half after Broadbent had equalised, scored it with a neat deliberate header from Meek's accurate lob. To get to the ball Forrest had to jump higher than McEvoy who, though not a notable header is a sturdy opponent. Forrest played him well and fed his wingers so intelligently that it is to be hoped he will be given an extended run at centre-forward.

United's attack, against a close-marking defence, was the best part of the team and might only be improved by the inclusion of Brook or Vickers at inside left. The current occupant of that position did little of note.

Meek's "goal"

Both sides had unlucky moments. The photographers at the end United were attacking in the first half said Meek scooped the ball over the goal-line before McIntosh was able to pounce on it and clear, and United's interval lead should therefore have been 2-0. Wednesday's misfortune came in the second half when Shiner beat the goalkeeper but saw his shot hit a full-back and disappear over the bar. Perhaps justice was done each time, for neither man should have missed scoring.

Wednesday would not have been flattered by a draw; United were not flattered by a win. it was a match which might well have resulted in one of three ways and by winning, United made the promotion issue wide open.

As Leeds' biggest star, John found himself in the headlines more than most. There was some interest in his family, but again the contrast with today is striking when you read a 1953 interview with his first wife, Peggy, where she explains that while he is away playing football, she prefers to "sit at home, knitting sweaters for John."

Much is made of the workload of modern footballers but it was certainly no easier half a century ago. Christmas would invariably mean matches on December 25 and Boxing Day - usually home and away against the same side, often at different ends of the country - as well as the Saturdays either side. Over Easter there were three games in four days.

Elland Road was far from the imposing stadium it is today. The West Stand was a worn-out wooden structure, soon to be destroyed by fire. Opposite, the Gelderd Road stand was equally dilapidated, providing little comfort under its corrugated iron roof. Behind one goal was the 'Scratching Shed' with its barrel-shaped, wooden roof, while the Kop area where the Revie stand is now, was a huge wind-swept cinder terrace with nothing to keep off the rain.

If the stadium was a far cry from the all-seater, comparative luxury experienced today, the pitch and equipment, too, bore little comparison. The playing area was more often than not a muddy, ploughed field with a little grass near each corner flag. On frosty days, you often had the bizarre contrast of one wing frozen solid while the other had thawed and was yielding.

Players' boots were built to last, covered the ankle and were made of a stiff leather which could take six months 'wearing in' accompanied by generous applications of Dubbin before you could complete 90 minutes without being crippled by blisters. But they needed to be solid because they were kicking a leather, panelled football that absorbed water and mud, and could become like a large cannon ball before a quarter of the game had passed. It was said that the most skilful wingers were not necessarily those who could dribble past a full-back and set up chances for team-mates, but those who could sling in a centre with the protruding lace facing goal so it didn't gash the centre-forward's head.

John smiles when he recalls those balls: "We had one goalkeeper at Leeds who, on a wet day, found it difficult to kick the thing out of the penalty area. If you got caught by one or headed it wrong, you would certainly feel it."

Perhaps a large part of John Charles's genius was that he could manipulate those balls as well as modern players perform with the lightweight balls of today. One contemporary, clearly still

Captain Fantastic:
John leads the team
out at Elland Road

A typically powerful penalty from
John leaves the 'keeper grasping air

dazzled, said: "John could chip the keeper perfectly on a day when most of us couldn't even get the ruddy thing out of the mud."

That talent was to be the decisive factor in Leeds' clinching promotion in 1956.

The season started with a 2-1 defeat at Barnsley followed by a couple of wins against Bury and Middlesbrough. But it was very much one step forward, one back. Raich Carter began with John at centre half and after eight games switched him to right-half where he could have a bit more influence on the build up of attacks. Young Jack Charlton came in as number five. But Leeds were still badly missing John's goals - he only had one to his name so far - and finally Carter decided they were more important than his presence in defence.

He must have had doubts after the first match when Leeds crashed 4-1 at Bristol Rovers but a Charles goal clinched the points in the following game against Stoke and he scored in each of the next five matches.

Not all those were victories but Leeds managed to keep in touch with a leadership where only Sheffield Wednesday were consistently good.

Carter again reshuffled his pack in mid-February for the visit of Wednesday, switching John to inside right, a midfield role where he could be more involved, help with the build-up as well as still getting forward to link up with the centre-forward. It paid off immediately. On a snow-covered pitch, he had what Dick Ulyatt described as "in many ways the best game Charles has ever played for Leeds United." Comparing his inside-forward play with that of manager, Raich Carter, in his pomp - heady praise indeed - Ulyatt described John that day as "the complete footballer in defence and attack." John put Leeds in front when he snapped up a rebound after Bob Forrest's shot was parried, and 5ft 10in Forrest climbed above the defence to head the winner.

At that stage there were still seven clubs in the hunt for promotion. Sheffield Wednesday remained hot favourites and it was a question of which of the chasing pack would put together the most consistent run. It was Leeds United.

A win over Plymouth was followed by an impressive Good Friday victory at Fulham. The following day, lacklustre Leeds went down 2-0 at Nottingham Forest, but that was all forgotten when a Charles hat-trick sparked a 6-1 Easter Monday crushing of Fulham, Johnny Haynes, Ron Greenwood, Jimmy Hill et al.

From then on there was no looking back and Carter proudly took them to his former club Hull on the final day of the season, knowing victory would mean promotion. Over 15,000 Leeds fans - 3,000 more than had watched the home win over Plymouth a month before - travelled to Boothferry Park and saw John head their side into the lead only for Hull to hit back quickly. Nerves were clearly playing a part and the game was in the last half-hour before Leeds were awarded a penalty. Up stepped Charles: "It was no easy task taking such an important kick, so I was doubly grateful when I saw the ball nestling in the back of the net," John later recalled.

Two late goals from veteran Harold Brook, signed for £600 from Sheffield United, finished off a run of six straight wins in which John had scored nine goals, taking his tally for the season to 29. At last he could display his talents on the big stage.

Leeds' return to the top flight for the first time since 1947 was against Everton at Elland Road on 18 August 1956 but, in those more constrained times, warranted only two paragraphs halfway down a general Yorkshire Post preview under the headline `Some League footballers still needed for cricket' and a picture of A Mitchell, 'signed for Southport and plays against Bradford City today.'

Of course there were those, especially in the south of England, who felt John Charles would find life much harder against top quality defences and he was eclipsed on the opening day, scoring

YORKSHIRE POST

MORNING EDITION   THE PRIDE OF YORKSHIRE   2ND APRIL 1956

United set the crowd roaring for more

Easter, as ever, proved a key time in the promotion race. A comfortable win at Craven Cottage on Good Friday was followed the next day by an indifferent performance at Nottingham Forest and a 2-0 defeat. Fulham's trip to Elland Road on 2 April 1956, Easter Monday, became even more important. Once more Big John rose to the situation.

Leeds United   6
Fulham   1
by ERIC STANGER

Down with a bump at Nottingham, Leeds United bounced back on the Second Division see-saw yesterday. Not only did they complete a holiday double over Fulham but scored their biggest win of the season, and once again put themselves in the thick of the promotion fight.

Any resemblance between United at Nottingham on Saturday and against Fulham both on Good Friday and at Elland Road yesterday, was purely coincidental. They snapped up their chances, set the crowd roaring for more, and generally looked a live promotion prospect.

Really they had the game in their pockets after the first half hour when they were three up with a stiffish breeze at their backs. They lost some accuracy and drive in the first quarter of an hour of the second half when the players developed an anxiety complex but recovered to win almost as they liked.

In top gear
Charles, after his rather indifferent display against the Forest, was back in top gear. He paved the way with a fine goal after six minutes when his 25-yard shot was so powerful that Black could only push the ball on to one post for it to

only once while 34-year-old Harold Brook snatched a hat-trick.

But by the end of the campaign John was the leading scorer in the league with 38 goals. Leeds finished eighth and he had scored against all the sides above them apart from Preston North End. He destroyed Sheffield Wednesday with three goals in both the home and away matches - a feat he had achieved against Rotherham in 1953-54 - taking his hat-trick tally for the club to 11.

In a season of great goals, perhaps the most memorable came at Elland Road on Boxing Day when Leeds beat championship hopefuls Blackpool 5-0. The Yorkshire Post reported: "A sensational opening set the home side on their victory march, the ball travelling in 13 seconds started off from the kick off, from Brook, Forrest and Overfield to Charles, who took the left winger's forward centre in his stride to crash the ball past Farm from the acutest of angles."

If those descriptions of Leeds' promotion campaign and their first season back in the First Division make you think of them as a one-man

ebound to the other, thence nto the net.

Nightingale, in his most ndustrious mood, got the econd by sheer persistence, haking Greenwood off the ball put United two up after 26 inutes, and Charles, with a rodigious leap to Meek's short ross, headed a third two inutes later. United were on elvet.

Haynes, whose distribution f the ball always bore the hall-ark of the class player, did rub e off with a quickly taken hance after 33 minutes, but ulham never looked like covering from those early ows. Three games in four days d taken more out of some of eir players than United's, it as apparent. Old dogs are good r hard roads - when they are ot too long.

econd scoring spurt

nited's second scoring spurt me in the last 20 minutes. rst Brook scored in a ramble, then Nightingale hit

Meek's centre past Black at the second attempt. With seven minutes left, Charles scored the goal of the game. Taking a free kick more than 20 yards out, after Nightingale had been fouled, he hit the ball into the back of the net like shell from a gun.

Black, so I am told, shouted to his defensive wall to part so that he would have clear sight of the ball. As he picked it out of the net, one disgruntled defender remarked: "Well did you see it?" I doubt it, but Black need not reproach himself. Goalkeepers - even the best of them - are beaten by such shots.

That goal was a fitting curtain. Charles showed that on top form whatever number he wears on his shirt he can stride the game like a Colossus. He just could not be kept out of this one. He was just as strong an influence in United's heartening win as Haynes was, with his quicksilver passes, in trying to keep Fulham in the game with a chance.

Jezzard off form

But Haynes had not the players alongside him that Charles had. The Fulham defence was very creaky under pressure, though Lowe worked himself almost to a standstill at left-half. Jezzard, never happy against Charlton, is right off form and nowhere near England rank.

United were always quicker to the ball and generally used it the better, especially from wing half where Gibson and Kerfoot also gave nothing away in defence.

It must have been a joy-day for the United crowd to see half a dozen goals coming from the forwards who showed refreshing purpose and dash, none more so than Meek who had his best game yet.

So United are still in the promotion hunt after Easter. They can keep there if they play as they have done in both games against Fulham - not if they play as at Nottingham. No doubt they know that.

team, you wouldn't be the first to think that. In some quarters they became known as 'John Charles United' - a tag John hated.

With typical sportsmanship he wrote in 'King of Soccer': "As far as the critics are concerned Leeds United did not seem to exist. They wrote about John Charles - they wrote about him so much that I had to stop keeping a scrapbook! But when they wrote about me they did not intend to give any publicity to the club or to my colleagues.

"But at Elland Road we twisted their praise. We refused to be led astray into the wilderness of individual praise. We were only concerned in winning praise for the team, and gaining publicity for the club. So when a heap of superlatives was showered upon me, we at Elland Road accepted the praise as collective praise for the whole team.

"It was absolutely scandalous to suggest that I did all the work for the Leeds United team. I had many fine colleagues and team-mates, and but for their unstinting loyalty and assistance I would never have gained my present position in football and neither would the club."

Those team-mates, however, were now going to have to do without John. After a single, memorable season in the First Division he was heading for Italy. But it had been a match for Wales that clinched that record-breaking deal.

Giants meet: John shakes hands with Sunderland skipper Don Revie, who was later to become manager at Leeds and re-sign John

THE ITALIAN JOB

For the final game of the Home International Championships in 1957 the Welsh selectors decided it was time to go with youth so, after being chosen for all 43 internationals since the war and playing in 41 of them, Alf Sherwood was dropped. John Charles was picked as skipper for the first time and as he led the side out at Windsor Park, Belfast, he was scrutinised from the stands by one of the wealthiest men in Europe.

Signor Umberto Agnelli was 22 years old, a member of the fabulously wealthy family which owned the Fiat car company. He concentrated on running Juventus Football Club which they also owned. He flew into Belfast to cast a final eye over the man they had been thinking of signing for over two years.

The first interest came from a dapper figure, Gigi Peronace, the agent whose brief was to scour Europe for the best players, especially those who could unlock the formidable Italian defences. He had already been responsible for the £35,000 move of Eddie Firmani from Charlton to Sampdoria.

It was Peronace who first identified John Charles as the perfect man for the job. John recalls:

"He came round my house and said he'd like me to go and play in Italy. He was a smashing feller who spoke very good English. He was nothing like the scouts who huddled on the touchlines in England. Gigi was a Lazio fan and wanted me to go there but a month later he came back and said he was now working for Juventus and I should join them."

News that Juventus were interested alerted some of the other big clubs around Europe and John found himself subject to endless rumours involving Real Madrid, Inter-Milan and other clubs who could afford what was bound to be massive fee.

The local paper was filled with correspondence, some saying Leeds should use the money to rebuild the team, others, like 'TB' of Armley, arguing: "We are now in grave danger of losing the city's greatest attraction since the Town Hall was built."

Things came to a head on 10 April 1957 when Leeds announced that, while they would not sell John to another club in England, they would not stand in his way if one of the big clubs in Europe came in for him.

Umberto Agnelli paused only long enough to tell the Yorkshire Evening Post: "We need Charles

KING JOHN

YORKSHIRE POST

MORNING EDITION   THE PRIDE OF YORKSHIRE   22ND APRIL 1956

'Experts' had predicted that John Charles would struggle in the top flight. Instead he flourished, becoming leading scorer with 38 goals and doing enough to persuade Juventus to pay a then-world record £65,000 for his services. His final game for Leeds before heading off to Turin was at Elland Road on 22 April 1957. Fittingly, Dick Ulyatt was in the Press box for the Yorkshire Post.

Leeds United   3

Sunderland   1

by RICHARD ULYATT

From a footballing point of view, John Charles could not have made a more fitting end to

Two spectacular goals for United to remember

his career at Elland Road. He scored the second and third goals United registered, making his total in the Football League this season 38 and he had to fight for every advantage he gained.

Sunderland badly needed the points. They could not allow Charles to have a spectacular match solely for sentiment's sake. Yet Charles did have a spectacular match.

I shall never forget the way in which he overtook Daniel, the upstanding Sunderland centre half, as they both raced towards the Sunderland goal and, as Daniel tried to keep the ball close to him, Charles

calmly stole it and without a check in his stride, without deviation.

It seemed as though one player merged into the other; red shirt was leading with the ball, suddenly a blue shirt was in front and there was no faltering. That was a new move in the Charles repertoire; I thought I had seen them all.

Opportunism

Both his goals were the reward of opportunism, both were scored only because an artist placed the ball. In each case he had to outpace the opposition.

For most of the match Charles suffered the unobtrusive

---

badly and we are determined to get him" before flying in to do the deal.

The transfer was thrashed out in room 233 of the Queens Hotel in Leeds. John remembers: "I walked to the hotel to meet the Italians and saw the Leeds directors Mr Bolton and Mr Westwood who were wearing black coats and black caps. Mr Bolton came up to me and said: `It's so sad that we're losing you, John' but as soon as they got the cheque they shot off to put it in the bank! When Umberto suggested we should have a drink to celebrate the deal, they were nowhere to be found."

The negotiations between the clubs were fairly straighforward. Juventus haggled for a while but even at £65,000 they thought they had a good deal.

Much tougher were the talks over personal terms held just along the corridor in room 222. For the first time a British player had employed the services of an agent to do the deal, and Teddy Sommerfield, used to negotiating with the BBC on behalf of people like Eamonn Andrews and Kenneth Wolstenholme, was well prepared and ready to strike a hard bargain. With Wolstenholme

Another great goal from Charles

marking of Daniel, who has played so often behind him for Wales that he must know his every move, of Anderson, Sunderland's inside right, and occasionally of Elliott who did nothing else of note. Yet Charles scored two goals.

He was set an example by the spectacular shot from 30 yards' range with which Harold Brook enlivened a match, often drab, to score the first goal after 55 minutes. The way Brook shoots from the middle of the field makes me wonder why United ever play him anywhere else than at centre-forward. It ended a neat passing bout.

Had O'Brien been in better shooting form - or had more luck - the score would have been more impressive, for this latest recruit to United's forward line hit two or three shots over the bar that ought to have gone under it. Yet he worked well; it was perhaps his best game so far.

Wood's saves

Sunderland so frequently mastered a shaky defence in which Dunn was much the most impressive figure that, but for the sound goalkeeping of Wood, they would have scored more than the goal Grainger gave them between Charles's first and second.

Wood made four saves of outstanding merit from a forward line too anxious to do the right thing quickly. Revie, except in finishing, was Sunderland's best player; inside left Clarke looked to be promising, but the defence was not good except for Fraser.

So the most remarkable season in United's history ended - a season which started with a newly promoted side almost reaching the top of the table, which was marked by a disastrous fire, by the wags christening it Charles United and by a transfer which involves £80,000.

Next season there will be no Charles to write about for the first time for nearly a decade. How odd it will seem. On recent form it is hard to say who will fill the gap.

there to help him on football matters, Sommerfield went through the contract item by item.

Downstairs the press were wondering what was going on - a player's contract usually took only ten minutes once the clubs had agreed. Twice refreshments were summoned to the room, brought by an awe-struck Italian waiter, who, once in, was reluctant to leave the scene of such important goings on.

Finally, agreement in principle was reached just after midnight but there was still plenty that could go wrong. John flew to Italy to approve the arrangements made for him and his family's accommodation in Turin. Then there was the matter of a medical, especially on those knees both of which had undergone cartilage operations. It was the most thorough examination John had experienced but the doctor, Professor Amilcare Basatti, declared: "Charles is the fittest man I know playing football, I have never seen a better human machine in a lifetime in medicine."

The biggest stumbling block was completely in Juventus's hands. They were facing the spectre of relegation and if that happened they would not

Juve's greatest-ever striker

Training with his new Juventus team-mates

be allowed to sign their new overseas star striker. Fortunately they just clung on to their senior status and the deal was done. John received £10,000 signing-on fee over the two year period of his first contract, a modest weekly salary but rich rewards in bonuses as well as a luxurious way of life. The 'Association Football Correspondent' of the Times recognised the importance of John's transfer. He wrote: "The implications of the move by Charles are as yet hidden. But after the departure of Firmani, an Italian by antecedant, from Charlton Athletic to Italy last year, it may one day prove a lever to greater incentives and rewards for the footballer at home." Four years later, after a massive campaign by the players union and a stand by George Eastham, the retain and transfer system was changed and the maximum wage in England was removed.

John's final game for Leeds United was against Sunderland at Elland Road. In his Yorkshire Post report, Geoffrey Winter waxed positively lyrical. Under the headline 'The Charles epoch comes to an end' he wrote: "John Charles left Leeds United's ground for the last time yesterday in a blaze of glory and trailing 100 small boys pleading for his autograph. So ended a chapter in football history, which will be told and retold as long as men wear Leeds United favour."

After telling of John's two fairy-tale goals, his 153rd and 154th for the club, Winter continued: "The black eyes of Signor Gigi Peronace, the Juventus scout, who was there to take delivery of John Charles when the match was over, glistened with excitement and satisfaction whenever the great man got possession of the ball. 'That's my boy,' they seemed to say...

"There was a disturbing incident in the Sunderland goalmouth in which Charles, running at his impressive top speed, collided with a player and hurtled to the ground at the back of the net. The goalkeeper was prone too. Trainers raced to give first-aid and someone shouted: 'He's broken a leg.' No-one imagined for one moment that he might be referring to the goalkeeper.

"Signor Peronace looked particularly anxious and was no doubt pale under his Mediterranean tan. Fortunately no serious harm was done to either player."

The end of one era marked the start of another, a five-year stay at Juventus in which John became an idol. In his first season he set the league alight with 29 goals and led the team that had nearly been relegated to the championship. He was voted Italian Footballer of the Year.

As Juventus entered one of their greatest periods, John formed a memorable partnership with the brilliant, if temperamental, Argentine Omar Sivori, whom he described as the best player he ever played alongside. In the five years of Charles's reign the club won three championships and twice collected the Italian Cup. John was honoured with a call-up to represent the Italian League.

Life in Italy could hardly have been more removed from that he had left behind in Leeds, both professionally and privately.

The rewards were great - John recalls that victory against Torino, Roma, Lazio or in other big games could see an extra £500 in the wage packet - but discipline was very strict. Article seven of the standard contract read: "The player must obey all the rules as to style and technique prescribed by the club and its officers; fix his place of residence where told by the club; always conduct himself in a correct manner everywhere and live a decent moral and physical life; conduct himself in an irreproachable manner sportingly and socially..." and so it runs on for several more clauses with the threat of a heavy fine if anyone overstepped the mark.

And players needn't think they could get away with anything without the club knowing. John said: "Everything you did was reported back. We often socialised with players from other clubs and I

Life at the top: John and his family enjoyed life in Italy

I Remember John

KENNETH WOLSTENHOLME was once the voice of football on television and his immortal words from the 1966 World Cup final 'They think it's all over..' - the title of his recently published autobiography - ensured him a place in broadcasting history. He is still actively involved in the game as part of Channel-4's team covering Italian soccer.

He got to know John Charles early in his career. They shared an agent - Teddy Sommerfield - and Kenneth 'ghosted' John's first two volumes of autobiography in 1957 and 1962. He was also involved in negotating John's move to Juventus.

"Teddy Sommerfield was quite a character. He acted as agent for me and Eamonn Andrews, sorting out contracts with the BBC and other things like books or personal appearances.

He met John and liked him and said he would act for him. He wasn't allowed to get involved in any of the football contracts in this country but he sorted out other deals for John. That must have made John one of the first footballers in England to have an agent.

When Juventus wanted him, Teddy said: 'You've got to be careful now, John. This is the big world and they can do anything with you.'

The thing I remember most was Teddy asking Juventus for a copy of a specimen contract that a player had to sign in the Italian league. They said they would get one translated for him but Teddy, who spoke Italian, said: 'Just send it to me in Italian.'

Teddy was a great negotiator. He liked football but he didn't know much about the inside of the game so he asked me to go up to Leeds with him so I could help him with any football matters.

He was Jewish with a tanned complexion. He looked Italian. We got off the train in Leeds and the porters said 'Don't help him, he's going to take our John!' but I assured them he was very much on John's side.

"This man used to score goals - he'd get you 20 or 30 a season - but he was also the finest centre half you could hope to have."

People always ask me who was the greatest player I've ever seen and I ask them what they mean - the greatest centre forward? greatest wingman?

I think the greatest all-round players I have ever seen are Alfredo di Stefano and John Charles.

In Italy they would agree with you but I don't think he's appreciated as much as he should be over here.

This man used to score goals - he'd get you 20 or 30 a season - but he was also the finest centre half you could hope to have. He was a tremendous guy. And he always played fairly.

The Italians said to him at one stage: 'Don't let them push you around. Knock them down.' To which John replied: 'If I've got to knock them down to beat them, I don't want to play.'

I remember we were filming Wales v England and twice John made great runs up the field with the ball. Wales won 2-1 but we ran out of film for both their goals and the people down there thought we wouldn't show it because Wales had won.

I shudder to think what he would be worth on the transfer market today. They talk about £40 million for David Beckham. What on earth would they want for John?"

remember coming into training just before a derby match and one of the directors saying `What were you doing out to dinner with Torino players last night?' They had spies everywhere."

At first John found the new training regime strange, especially the pre-season camp up in the mountains which he described as being like "living in a monastery." For the first time part of his training included relaxing, something he never came to terms with: "I was always bored to tears with these pre-season jaunts," he wrote in The Gentle Giant. "I was sick of sitting around doing nothing. I was sick of writing letters. I was sick of reading or playing cards or billiards. To me it didn't rest my mind or my body. It just made me more nervous, more jumpy."

The other side of the coin was to live a lifestyle only film stars could emulate. John adds: "We had a luxury apartment in the hills and when the kids were on holiday for three months in the summer, my wife would take them down to the coast and I would join them whenever I had some time off.

"Everyone wanted to know you. Sophia Loren was a Juventus fan and we often found ourselves in her company. People would buy you drinks and meals, and you were treated well wherever you went. Mind, the ordinary fans could turn against you pretty quickly. There was one cafe we used to go in

John is chaired off the pitch by Juventus fans after they clinched their tenth championship in 1958

Juventus skipper Boniperti tries a Juventus shirt for size against the big frame of his new team-mate

where the fans would come just to see you and offer to buy you coffee, but if we had lost, it was empty."

It is difficult, forty years on, to convey the impact the quiet Welshman had on football-obsessed Turin but perhaps the fact that his fame is celebrated today on the newest of media, the internet, is testament enough.

On the official Juventus website there is a page headed 'John Charles: Juve's finest ever forward'. It reads: "Devastating is the adjective that springs to mind when you recall the power of Welsh international John Charles. Charles was the greatest - and not only in terms of stature - centre-forward in Juventus history. World-class strikers have come and gone. Deserving of special mention here are `Farfallino' Borel, John Hansen, 'Bobby-go!' Bettega, Jose Altafini, Petruzzu Anastasi and Paulo Rossi. They were all great in their own right but there was no-one quite like Charles.

"For anyone who saw Charles play in the late 1950s and early 1960s when he was at his peak, the

Welshman was the stuff of legends. There is a famous photo of him scoring yet another header and the goalkeeper is clinging on to him while two defenders try in vain to stop him. Another picture shows the dreadnought striker leaping above Vieri in a derby match and even at full stretch, the Torino keeper is nowhere near him.

"John Charles was more than the proverbial battering-ram. He was blessed with the ability to hang in the air and, as if suspended in motion, he would use his momentary advantage to decide whether to head for goal or lay the ball off for a colleague to apply the coup de grace. His unselfish play won him many admirers."

The other aspect of John's play which the Italians particularly noted was the fact that he never used his power to gain an unfair advantage. One of Italy's leading football writers, Giancarlo Galavotti, described John as: "Part and parcel of the greatest of the greatest days of Italian football...His enormous goal-scoring talent inspired the fantasies and adulation of the fans who called him 'Gigante Buono', the Gentle Giant.

"The name was inspired by not only his powerful play and physical appearance but also by his character and conduct on the field...He was regarded as the epitome of the British gentleman."

John's was simply the biggest star in Turin. He made a best-selling record, starred in a film with Sivori, owned a share of a restaurant, and was feted wherever he went. But after four years he decided the time was coming when he would want to return home so, despite tremendous pressure from Juventus, he signed only a one-year extension to his contract and announced that he would return to the Football League. In all John played 155 games for Juventus, scoring 108 goals.

When word got back to Leeds, where the club was back in the Second Division, that their favourite son might be coming back, the pressure on the board to find the cash to sign him became intense.

I Remember John

JOHN MORGAN spent over 50 years in the newspaper business in Leeds, in which time he became a close friend of John Charles, and on many occasions 'ghosted' articles for the giant Welshman. A doyen of the after-dinner speaking circuit, John Morgan was delighted to pay his own tribute to a Leeds United legend:

"When you ask John Charles to name the best football player he has no hesitation in nominating Alfredo Di Stefano.

It is a compliment returned by many who believe that John was the greatest soccer export from Britain to Europe.

Charles still enjoys God-like status in Italy, and today he walks tall in the streets of Leeds with a lack of affectation, sheer modesty, and the dignity which will never desert his towering stature.

The man Italians called Il Buon Gigante, the Gentle Giant, sampled the heady delights of the champagne jet set, with a luxurious home in the breathtaking surroundings of Turin.

According to John Charles, Alfredo Di Stefano was the best

He had a hideaway in the mountain region, a seaside chalet, top of the range vehicle, and the passionate adulation of thousands of fans.

Charles had shares in a nightclub and restaurant, and a hit record, 'Sixteen Tons', in the pop charts. He was feted, bedecked in football honours, and enjoyed the security and peace of mind which comes with a healthy bank balance.

Today he lives in a comparatively humble detached and rented house in Birkenshaw, near Bradford, where the immaculate interior displays only a couple of reminders of his life as 'Roy of the Rovers.'

The medals, caps, trophies and trappings of a world acclaimed football hero have gone, either given away, sold, or donated to charitable causes.

'King John', like another monarch, lost his brand of the crown jewels although he still retains an impish sense of humour and a booming laugh which lightens his face and restores a gleam to his eyes.

He said: "I was a good footballer. People tell me I was great. But I was also the worst businessman.

"The breaking up of marriage to my first wife Peggy cost me a lot of money. I ploughed fortunes into a disastrous sports shop venture in Cardiff and, when I returned from Italy, inflation set in and I was close to financial ruin."

John added with a mischievous grin: "I'm proud of the fact that I speak fluent Italian. But I never bothered to master the words for 'sick as a parrot' and I don't intend to start now."

The rise from rags to riches and back to modest means was started in 1949 when the 16-year-old arrived at Leeds United from Cwmdu, Swansea. He was on Swansea Town's groundstaff for two years without getting a game.

Leeds United boss Major Frank Buckley offered the teenager a £10 signing on fee, £6 a week, and a new suit and overcoat as a bonus.

The late Tom Holley was captain and asked Major Buckley to rest him because he felt a little jaded. Tom suggested that the manager should 'give the big lad in the second team a game.'

It was a mistake on Tom's part. Within four minutes of John making his first team debut, Tom confided to a colleague on the bench: 'My football days are over!'

John quickly became the Elland Road idol - a dominant centre-half and a superb striker and header of the ball as a free-scoring centre forward.

There was no more majestic sight in soccer than to see him striding for goal with the ball destined to thud into the opposition net. He was powerful, clean, fair, and never booked or sent off. He was simply the best.

John was transferred to Juventus for a record fee of £65,000 and he was offered £18 a week in wages which was £2 less than he received at Leeds. He explained: "I didn't mind the cut in salary because our win bonus was generous and scorers received extra cash for goals."

He slotted in 122 in five years, helping Juventus to three championships, and it was estimated that he earned over £100,000 - the equivalent of more than £1m today.

John has little more than memories of his halcyon sporting days and he recalls that he was reluctant to leave Elland Road but quickly settled in the land of the lira.

He said: "There was a lot of heart-searching because British soccer at that time was the best and most exciting in the world.

"Italian fans are wonderful and probably the greatest of all was a Juventus follower whose love of the side was an obsession.

"Before one match he hollered: 'Big John, look at my wife. She is dressed in the Juventus colours.' And with that he clawed his embarrassed wife's dress up to her neck to reveal black and white striped pants and bra.

"Believe it or not that lady was under orders to wear black and white over garments and under garments every day of her life. And she did, otherwise she might have been black and blue. Her husband was a bit of a bully."

John's British buddies in Italy at that time were Denis Law, who was also an idol, Jimmy Greaves and Joe Baker.

John said: "Joe had a little trouble in fitting in and he will forgive me for saying that he depended to a great extent on Denis's skill.

"They were magical days. Presents for footballers were lavish. Fiat often gave cars to players as win bonuses, and in one spell of dinners

There was no more majestic sight in soccer than to see him striding for goal with the ball destined to thud into the opposition net.

"But the promise of security, glorious days in the golden sunshine, and a new life for my wife and three boys was irrisistible.

"I had the chance to play for Italy but refused to represent that country at international level. The decision cost me money, several Italian friends, and perhaps soccer prestige. But my Welsh pride and my pride in British football would not allow me to play for another country."

John learned to cope with fanatical fan worship but it meant that he could not lead a normal life, taking the family to the local shopping areas or even for an afternoon stroll.

He said: "Peggy and the boys - Terry, Melvyn and Peter - were mobbed and swarmed over by supporters. There was never a hint of violence just a demonstration of loyalty, affection and hero worship.

"There were times when we ached for privacy and specially when Juventus were beaten in a crucial match by Turin and I missed a penalty which would have drawn the game.

and receptions, I was presented with 15 gold medals."

It was an unbelieveable transition for the shy young man from Swansea, via Leeds, to a fabulous world in Italy, and he was entitled to be overwhelmed by the extravagant largesse dispensed by those who governed football clubs.

After Juventus clinched one Italian championship, celebrations drew to a dawn finale with one leading player receiving a priceless gold watch from a director. He removed it from his wrist, slapped it in the hand of the grateful player and said: 'You deserve more. You will sleep with my friend.'

The friend turned out to be an internationally known film star - still alive today - and she entertained the player for a month.

John was also at a post-match party when the wine flowed and one of his team mates decided that he would end the evening on an amorous note. The club chairman was appraised of the situation and squired his two beautiful daughters throughout the protracted celebrations.

The chairman did his chaperone job exceedingly well but it was noticed that the love sick player had disappeared. He was missing for an hour.

When he returned, he wore a smug and satisfied smile and when John asked him where he had been, he grinned: "The chairman has been looking after his daughters. And I have been looking after his wife."

John struck up a friendship with the Argentine Omar Sivori who the Welshman regarded as "a superb footballing wizard with immense skill and talent."

John added: "He was the best I had the privilege to partner but he had a terrible temper which often touched flashpoint and it was better to keep out of his way.

"He was also the ugliest player and when he scored, we didn't kiss him - we ran to the other side of the pitch.

"But he had more skill in his little finger than many had in their bodies. I once saw him toe-end a table tennis ball over 200 times without it touching the floor. He could do the same with heavy iron bowls used in the Italian equivalent of our bowling game.

"Omar played with his socks around his ankles and his unprotected legs were subjected to the most vicious tackles. But he could evade a Sherman tank and his goal scoring was prolific.

"We scored 250 goals between us in five seasons and he didn't live off me. He was a truly great player in his own right."

John experienced the intrusion of the Mafia into football. One morning he responded to the urgent knocking of his hotel bedroom door to find a couple of sinister looking chaps asking for Sivori.

John woke his room mate and the Argentinian left the room to join the men. When he returned he pretended he had hurt his leg and would not be able to play. He then confessed that he had been threatened with the loss of his life if he scored.

Sivori was prevailed on to play but he constantly eyed the packed stands in search of a glint from a gun.

Suddenly the ball was crossed, struck Sivori on the back of the head and went into the net. The Juventus players formed a scrum round him, walked him crablike to the tunnel, and the match proceded. By this time Sivori was on the next plane back to Turin.

The opposition eventually equalised and the game was heading for a draw until John received the ball and darted between two advancing fullbacks. They collided and John went on to hit the 'winning goal.'

The referee's whistle sounded and he shouted 'offside.' John protested and said to the whistler: 'How on earth can it be offside when two players came forward to tackle me?' The referee replied: 'Like Mr Sivori, I too have to get home safely.'

John's memories of Italy would fill a book on their own and, like many soccer and other sporting legends, he is living through a never-ending anti-climax.

He recalls with a touch of nostalgia those days of high ambition and supreme achievement. But he is now committed to days of ordinary survival.

Having recovered from the threat of cancer, he is content to follow breakfast with an attempt to solve his newspaper's crossword, hours before the television set, and the occasional sortie to Peter Lorimier's pub, The Commercial in Holbeck Village, Leeds.

His presence at sporting dinners is always welcomed and invariably results in a standing ovation. His occasional trips to Italy are highlights in an otherwise humdrum existence.

He left football management to become landlord at the New Inn, Churwell, not far from the Leeds United ground. He and his wife Glenda also ran the Gomersal Park Hotel on the outskirts of the city but this occupation folded - a kind of 'late tackle' at the wrong time of his life.

John is an honoured 'old boy' and regular at Elland Road. he is a member of the Leeds United ex-Players' Association and keeps in touch with his old soccer friends and colleagues.

He will sing 'Sixteen Tons' at the drop of a hat and is a man revered by those who saw his inimitable brand of soccer magic.

They will continue to regale those who were not fortunate enough to see him in glorious action with tales of his prowess and dynamic shooting.

Il Buon Gigante is a legend - a giant sized version."

END OF AN ERA

Several clubs wanted the 31-year-old striker's signature including some in the First Division, but the lure of Leeds was still strong for John. Don Revie, an opponent many times on the field, had taken over as manager and was building a promotion-winning team around the experience of Bobby Collins and the emerging talent of Billy Bremner. Chairman Harry Reynolds put season tickets on sale for the 1962-3 season with a note that said: "There may be the possibility of Charles coming back, in which case there may be an increase in price" and sure enough, when Leeds paid £53,000 for their former star that August, the prices went up.

But the excitement among the fans was such that most didn't even object to that. The Yorkshire Evening Post gave supporters the chance to write a 'welcome home' message in 25 words and were inundated with thousands of them, many in verse. The winner of the two guineas for the best went to Mrs A Sunderland of Leeds, who found inspiration from the Bard for her entry:

"Come four divisions of the League in arms,
We shall shock them, naught shall make us rue,
If Leeds United to King John be true!"

Others were rooted more down to earth. With a Yorkshireman's eye on't brass, Mr B Armer of Hull wrote:

"Tha'rt costing us varry dear,
Aye, US - WE'RE carrying t'load,
But if tha shoves us up next year
Tha'rt more na welcome at Elland Road."

The expectations of a miracle were high. One person wrote that he had "never seen a game at Elland Road since you left, but now the magnet is back...so am I" and the headline of the John Charles Special edition, priced threepence, screamed: "He's back again. 1956 .. Division One, 1957 .. Italy, 1962-63 .. ?"

Living up to the hype would have been hard enough at his peak but John had missed pre-season training and was overweight and far from at his physical best. The English game was all hustle and bustle, and long balls for people to chase, a million miles from what he had become used to in Italy.

In The Gentle Giant he admitted: "I turned out for Leeds when I wasn't match-fit, and every move I made was in the glare of publicity from television, radio and newspapers. Publicity is fine when you are doing well, but I knew in my heart of hearts that I wasn't playing well."

John wasn't happy with the game he was expected to play as Leeds tried to scrap their way to the top flight. He believed football "is played with players moving into spaces, moving close to the man with the ball. And it is not played at a breakneck speed all the time. For the first time in my life I worried about my football at Leeds. I realised that I just could not get used to it. And the more I worried, the worse I played."

John played only 11 league games, scoring three goals in a 91-day stay before he was sold to Roma for £70,000. He handled the situation with typical politeness, saying: "I'm sorry it has turned out like this because I had looked forward to coming back to Leeds. It proved a mistake."

Back in Italy he scored within 15 minutes of his debut for Roma against Bologna before flying back to play his last match for Leeds United, a friendly against Juventus which had been arranged as part of the deal that took him from Turin to Elland Road.

Injury and a loss of form meant the stay in the Eternal City lasted only one season after which George Swindin, manager at Cardiff City, snapped John up for a bargain £20,000. Even though he was still playing well enough to be called up for his country, John doesn't recall his return to Wales as an especially good part of his career. But after three seasons at Ninian Park, he took over as player-manager at Hereford United, a position he enjoyed greatly.

His presence attracted large crowds and he put down the foundations that led to the Edgar Street club being elected to the Football League. He brought through some young players and blended them with a few seasoned pros.

John recalls: "Things went very well and most of the team that went into the league and had their famous FA Cup run were my players. But eventually the chairman wanted to run things and I decided it was time to get out. At one stage I had thought I would learn the manager's trade at Hereford before moving on to a bigger club but I decided management wasn't for me. I enjoyed the coaching - we were part time so we used to train on Tuesdays and Thursdays - but I wasn't keen on the office work and didn't particularly like having to tell players they were left out of the team."

There followed a brief spell as manager of Merthyr Tydfil, where John still turned out at the age of 41. "I loved it there. We were in the Southern League and I remember Ken Brown, who used to play at West Ham, came down and joined me. It was wonderful to think we were doing something for the town. The crowds went up from five hundred to over two thousand, so we must have been doing something right."

When John finally hung up his boots, it seemed natural to find his way back to his adopted home of Leeds where he has lived ever since. Strange to say he is still less recognised as he goes around Leeds than he is on his trips back to Turin and Rome, where 'Giovanni' is soon invited in for a glass of wine and to talk football. Juventus have never forgotten his contribution to their history and fly him over for special occasions and made made him a guest of honour when they reached the European Cup final.

Leeds United held a testimonial for John and Bobby Collins in 1988 and since chairman/fan Peter Ridsdale took charge of the club, there are

Don Revie looks on as John Charles re-signs for Leeds, but the move was short lived

By 1964 and after a spell with Roma in Italy, Charles faced his old side in the colours of Cardiff City

signs that John's place in its history is at last getting full recognition.

He still goes regularly to Elland Road to watch matches. "I was a big admirer of the team that Don Revie produced in the sixties and seventies and wonder if I'd stayed longer when I came back from Juventus if I would have played a part in that. I would have like that."

John sees a lot of similarities with the team that David O'Leary is creating at the start of the 21st century. "He's bringing together a good crop of youngsters at the same time and letting them develop together. I enjoy watching them."

A series of business failures and rampant inflation meant John's lifestyle has often been comparatively modest, especially when seen beside that of the majority of modern players, who will never come anywhere near matching his ability. But he expresses no bitterness and is renowned for his generosity in fund raising for charity.

He scarcely has a memento left, having answered endless requests for 'something for the auction'. He can't even find his championship medals from Juventus and guesses that at some stage he gave them away. Perhaps one of his friends expressed it best when he claimed: "John lacked the one gift needed to get by in a world of wolves - cynicism."

But it's not a matter of regret for the modest Welshman. He just smiles and says: "I've got my memories and I've got my friends. That's what's really important. I don't need medals and caps to remind me of what I've done."

And the Gentle Giant has something that few modern footballers in their mansions and fast cars will ever have: the name of John Charles will be mentioned among the great players for as long as football is discussed. He has the right to be spoken of in the same sentence as Pele, Cruyff and Di Stefano. He is truly King John.

I Remember John

KEN JONES has been one of Britain's top sports writers for over 30 years. A former professional footballer, he has followed John Charles's career from its early days. Here we reproduce an article he wrote for the Independent to mark John's 65th birthday in 1996.

"History rewritten. Sweden 1958. John Charles causes a sensation with a marvellous header that sends Brazil out of the World Cup. In truth, Brazil defeated Wales 1-0 in the quarter-finals with a goal fluked by the 17-year-old Pele and went on to win the tournament - but what if Charles had been able to turn out?

The particular target for violent tackling when Wales played off against Hungary for a place in the last eight, Charles failed a fitness test shortly before the game. 'With John out there we would have won.' the late Jimmy Murphy, who managed Wales when Matt Busby's assistant at Manchester United, always maintained.

So does Cliff Jones: 'They were all terrified of John,' the former Tottenham Hotspur winger said, 'Brazil included. A magnificent all-round footballer, tremendous in the air. We got in some pretty good centres that day, Terry Medwin from the right, me from the left, and with all respect for Colin Webster who was brought into the team, I still think about what John might have done with them.'

Hard to believe, but Charles will be 65 on Friday. A pensioner. 'You're bloody right. It's frightening how quickly the years pass,' he said when we spoke recently at his home in Birkenshaw, West Yorkshire. 'Where did they go? It seems only like yesterday since...'

Only like yesterday since he was in the Leeds United first team at just 17, capped by Wales before his 19th birthday; since a transfer to Juventus in 1957 led to him becoming a revered figure in Italian football.

We were sitting in the front room of a modest but comfortable semi-detached house where Charles lives with his second wife, Glenda, and it was about four o'clock in the afternoon. Charles was sitting in an easy chair, gazing at a coal fire. He had on dark slacks and a black sweater, and he was smoking a cigarette. He looked massive.

I was watching Charles. I was watching him sit there as though he could see something in the flames that I couldn't. This is a guy, I was thinking to myself, who is far away, a guy remembering how it used to be, the excitement of that first season at Juventus when his 28 league goals inspired them to the Italian championship.

My question broke the silence. 'Do you ever regret coming back,' I asked, 'not making a life out there?'

Charles smiled. 'Sometimes,' he said.

He knew what I meant. Here the legend does not serve Charles well but even for the younger generation of Italian football supporters he is an heroic figure. 'Gianni (Gianni Agnelli, the Fiat magnate and head of the family that owns Juventus) looked after many of the old players, set them up in business,' he added, 'and although we didn't part on the best of terms I knew I could have gone back. My big mistake was leaving Juventus in the first place, because once the link was broken things could never be same.'

In August 1962, his first marriage on the slide, and concerned for his children, Charles returned to play again for Leeds. A mistake. Three months later he was back in Italy turning out for Roma. Another mistake. At odds with Roma's coach, beset by injuries, he made only 10 appearances, lost his place in the Wales team and was sold to Cardif City at the end of that season. There followed spells in non-League football as player-manager of Hereford and Merthyr Tydfil. Then it was over.

Imagine, though, a man standing 6ft 2in and weighing around 13st, with a huge torso rising from narrow hips to broad shoulders; with terrific balance, effortless touch and the spring of a high jumper. Brave too. No wonder the good judges put Charles among the 10 greatest players in history and alongside Geoge Best in the annals of British football.

Maybe Charles is the best British player of all time. I don't know. There is no exact way of measuring such a thing but within a year of joining Juventus he was considered to be the leading player in Europe, ahead even of the Real Madrid maestro, Alfredo di Stefano.

Darkness was drawing in, the fire began to cast shadows. Charles's voice startled me: 'You know something,' he said, 'I expected to sign for Lazio. Gigi (Gigi Peronace, who acted as agent for Italian clubs) had the deal lined up but then, typically, he brought in Juventus. Gianni's younger brother,

Charles chortled: 'Sometimes when I think about the people who gave me a bashing, I regret not bashing them back. But it's nice to know that I went through my career without hurting anybody.'

Never an easy touch though. 'The big fella sells himself short,' Charlton said one night. 'Calm, yes, but nobody got the ball off him without a struggle. He was quick over the ground, exceptionally strong, and kept his elbows out so wide it was difficult to get in close. He had a powerful shot and, in the air, well, he was on his own, different class. There are some pretty useful performers in that department around today, and people have told me about Dixie Dean and Tommy Lawton, what great headers of the ball they were, scoring from as far out as the edge of the penalty area, but I can't imagine they were better than John. Going for crosses he would jump a second before you and thrust his chest into your shoulders. Most players close their eyes instinctively but I've seen pictures of John heading the ball with his eyes wide open.'

We were reminiscing. A day or so after Charles arrived in Turin he bought a car. A Citroen. 'I didn't

"If he was playing, there were always thousands extra on the gate. People wanted to see him play."

Umberto - the club's president - came to watch me play for Wales against Northern Ireland in Belfast, and that was it.'

Jack Charlton, who was then making his way at Leeds, had no doubts that Charles would be a success in Italy. 'In those days I didn't know much about the game over there but John would have made it anywhere,' he said. 'Whenever I'm asked at dinners about the most effective British player of my time I'm sure people expect me to say Best or our kid (Bobby), but they forget about John. While everybody else just played the game he went out and won matches on his own.'

A placid temperament thwarting all attempts at provocation - he was never sent off or cautioned and scorned petty fouling - Charles would become known as Il Buon Gigante - 'the Gentle Giant'.

I remember the late Dave Bowen, who captained Arsenal and Wales, saying that it was frightening to think of the damage Charles could have done with his tremendous strength if he had been a bully.

think,' he chuckled. 'Right away Gianni was on the telephone asking what I was trying to do to him. All the players got Fiats anyway.'

Some felt Charles had no peers at centre-half, the position he first filled at Leeds. Others that he was the complete centre-forward.

I had never heard him state a preference. 'So which was it?' I asked.

'Centre-forward,' he replied. 'No question. A defender can kick five shots off the line but goalscorers get the glory.'

There was plenty of that. Charles scored 97 League goals for Juventus in 165 matches. Striking up a devastating partnership with the fiery litle Argeninian inside-forward Omar Sivori, who became his friend, Charles scored 23 times in the 1959-60 season when Juventus won another championship and the cup, winning it with a record of 55 points and 92 goals.

At the mention of Sivori's name, Charles chuckled: 'Strange little bugger,' he said. 'We were pals from the start and Gianni loved him. He was always telling hm that there was no better inside-forward in the world, so when Inter signed Luis Suarez from Barcelona, and his wages were printed in the newspapers, I knew there would be an explosion. Sivori was furious and he persuaded me to go with him to see Gianni. He asked for his contract and tore it up. Gianni just smiled at him, 'Here's your new contract,' he said, handing it over.'

'And you, John,' I said, 'something for you?'

'No,' he replied. 'It never came up, and you know me, I was never one for making trouble.'

Would I believe a weekly wage of £18, two pounds less than the maximum then permitted in English football?

'You're kidding,' I said. 'That's the truth,' he replied. 'Mind you, I got £10,000 to sign and we got big bonuses. No tax either. Gianni handled that. I remember him coming into the dressing room one day and drawing a line down through the map of Italy. 'I pay the tax on this side,' he said. Amazing people the Agnellis, so rich, so powerful. One time, Umberto came on the bus after we'd beaten AC Milan to say that he'd won a big bet with their president. Next thing he hands over a cheque to Boniperti. Came to about 800 quid each.'

A villa on the Italian Riviera, part owner of a restaurant, making records and a film with Sivori, the big Welshman had it all including widespread admiration.

Making a rare appearance at centre-half in a win over Torino, he injured one of their players. 'I'd won the ball and seeing the gap that opened up, our supporters were shouting for me to go through and score. But when I glanced behind me, the player I'd tackled was lying on the floor. I stopped and kicked the ball out of play so he could get some treatment.'

'Can't image that went down very well,' I said, not associating Corinthian attitudes with Italian football.

'Nobody mentioned it,' Charles replied, 'but late that night there was a din outside our villa. Horns going, people shouting. I looked out and saw this line of cars full of Torino supporters waving their red scarves. When I went and asked what it was all about one of them came forward and said that they wanted to thank me for what I'd done. I invited them in, about 20 all told, and by the time they left in the early hours of the morning they had drunk all my wine.'

Through a family connection Charles almost began his career with Leyton Orient. Instead he went on to the ground staff at Swansea and was spirited away by a Leeds scout who lived around the corner from the Vetch Field.

So long ago. So many memories. So many great moments. Maybe too much nostalgia. Charles spends much of his time in the company of old Leeds players Peter Lorimer, Billy Bremner and Bobby Collins. They raise money for charity and sometimes Charles is asked to speak at dinners.

Sadly there wasn't enough support for a function to celebrate his 65th birthday. Surely they haven't forgotten the man of whom Jimmy Murphy said: 'Whenever I look at him, it is as though the Messiah has returned'."

KING JOHN

John Charles's career at Leeds United

DATE	OPPONENT	H/A	COMP	SCORE	NO	ATT	GOALS
1948-49 Season							
23/04/49	Blackburn Rvrs	A	Lge 2	0-0	5	18,873	
30/04/49	Cardiff City	H	Lge 2	0-0	5	19,945	
07/05/49	QPR	A	Lge 2	0-2	5	16,730	
Leeds finished 15th in Division Two							
1949-50 Season							
20/08/49	QPR	H	Lge 2	1-1	5	31,589	
22/08/49	West Ham	A	Lge 2	1-3	5	24,728	
27/08/49	Preston N E	A	Lge 2	1-1	5	31,378	
31/08/49	West Ham	H	Lge 2	2-2	5	29,732	
03/09/49	Swansea T	A	Lge 2	1-2	5	29,767	
05/09/49	Sheffield Utd	A	Lge 2	1-0	5	22.126	
10/09/49	Tottenham H	A	Lge 2	0-2	5	48,274	
14/09/49	Sheffield Utd	H	Lge 2	0-1	5	23,199	
17/09/49	Southampton	A	Lge 2	1-2	5	23,214	
24/09/49	Coventry City	H	Lge 2	3-3	5	22,590	
01/10/49	Luton	A	Lge 2	0-1	5	15,291	
08/10/49	Cardiff City	H	Lge 2	2-0	5	25,523	
15/10/49	Blackburn Rvrs	A	Lge 2	1-0	5	22,038	
22/10/49	Brentford	H	Lge 2	1-0	5	27,342	
29/10/49	Hull City	A	Lge 2	0-1	5	47,638	
05/11/49	Sheffield Wed	H	Lge 2	1-1	5	33,733	
12/11/49	Plymouth A	A	Lge 2	2-1	5	21,923	1 pen
19/11/49	Chesterfield	H	Lge 2	0-0	5	24,409	
26/11/49	Bradford	A	Lge 2	2-1	5	18,401	
03/12/49	Leicester City	H	Lge 2	1-1	5	26,768	
10/12/49	Bury	A	Lge 2	0-2	5	13,381	
17/12/49	QPR	A	Lge 2	1-1	5	13,256	
24/12/49	Preston N E	H	Lge 2	3-1	5	41,303	
26/12/49	Barnsley	A	Lge 2	1-1	5	27,017	
27/12/46	Barnsley	H	Lge 2	1-0	5	47,817	
31/12/49	Swansea T	A	Lge 2	2-1	5	23,192	
07/01/50	Carlisle Utd	A	FAC3	5-2	5	22,832	
14/01/50	Tottenham H	H	Lge 2	3-0	5	50,476	
21/01/50	Southampton	H	Lge 2	1-0	5	38,646	
28/01/50	Bolton W	H	FAC4	1-1	5	51,488	
01/02/50	Bolton W	A	FAC4R	3-2aet	5	29,440	
04/02/50	Coventry City	A	Lge 2	4-0	5	22,990	
11/02/50	Cardiff City	H	FAC5	3-1	5	53,099	
18/02/50	Luton T	H	Lge 2	2-1	5	37,263	
25/02/50	Cardiff City	A	Lge 2	0-1	5	28,423	
04/03/50	Arsenal	A	FAC5	0-1	5	62,273	
11/03/50	Brentford	A	Lge 2	0-0	5	22,231	
18/03/50	Hull City	H	Lge 2	0-0	5	49,465	
25/03/50	Sheffield Wed	A	Lge 2	2-5	5	50,485	
01/04/50	Bradford	H	Lge 2	0-0	5	31,062	
07/04/50	Grimsby	A	Lge 2	0-2	5	22,511	
08/04/50	Leicester City	A	Lge 2	1-1	5	33,881	
10/04/50	Grimsby	H	Lge 2	1-0	5	17,991	
15/04/50	Plymouth A	H	Lge 2	1-1	5	24,132	
22/04/50	Chesterfield	A	Lge 2	1-3	5	11,346	
26/04/50	Blackburn Rvrs	A	Lge 2	2-1	5	12,538	
29/04/50	Bury	H	Lge 2	4-1	5	8,913	
Leeds finished 5th in Division Two							
West Riding Sen Cup							
06/05/50	Bradford City	A	WRSC	2-3	5	14,372	
1950-51 Season							
19/08/50	Doncaster Rvrs	H	Lge 2	3-1	5	40,208	
21/08/50	Coventry City	A	Lge 2	0-1	5	30,213	
02/09/50	Blackburn	H	Lge 2	0-1	5	32,799	
07/09/50	Swansea T	A	Lge 2	2-4	5	19,501	
09/09/50	Southampton	A	Lge 2	0-2	5	25,806	
16/09/50	Barnsley	H	Lge 2	2-2	5	37,633	
23/09/50	Sheffield Utd	A	Lge 2	2-2	5	28,872	
30/09/50	Luton T	H	Lge 2	2-1	5	21,209	
07/10/50	Bury	H	Lge 2	1-1	5	28,859	
14/10/50	Preston N E	A	Lge 2	0-2	5	35,578	
21/10/50	Chesterfield	H	Lge 2	2-0	5	23,032	
28/10/50	QPR	A	Lge 2	0-3	5	15,935	
04/11/50	Manchester City	H	Lge 2	1-1	5	30,764	
11/11/50	Leicester City	A	Lge 2	5-1	5	26,573	
18/11/50	Notts County	H	Lge 2	0-1	5	29,728	
25/11/50	Grimsby	A	Lge 2	2-2	5	15,561	
02/12/50	Birmingham City	H	Lge 2	3-0	5	23,355	
09/12/50	Cardiff City	A	Lge 2	0-1	5	23,716	
16/12/50	Doncaster Rvrs	A	Lge 2	4-4	5	16,745	
23/12/50	Brentford	H	Lge 2	1-0	5	19,839	
25/12/50	West Ham Utd	A	Lge 2	1-3	5	19,519	
26/12/50	West Ham Utd	H	Lge 2	2-0	5	33,162	
06/01/51	Middlesbrough	H	FAC3	1-0	5	45,583	
13/01/51	Southampton	H	Lge 2	5-3	5	29,253	
20/01/51	Barnsley	A	Lge 2	2-1	5	21,967	
27/01/51	Manchester Utd	A	FAC4	0-4	5	55,434	
03/02/51	Sheffield Utd	H	Lge 2	1-0	5	28,438	
24/02/51	Bury	A	Lge 2	1-0	5	13,517	
03/03/51	Preston N E	H	Lge 2	0-3	5	42,114	
10/03/51	Chesterfield	A	Lge 2	0-1	5	9,956	
17/03/51	QPR	H	Lge 2	2-2	5	18,094	
23/03/51	Hull City	A	Lge 2	0-2	5	46,701	
24/03/51	Manchester City	A	Lge 2	1-4	9	35,149	
26/03/51	Hull City	H	Lge 2	3-0	9	27,887	2
07/04/51	Notts County	A	Lge 2	0-0	5	23,466	
14/04/51	Grimsby	H	Lge 2	1-0	9	15,524	1
Leeds finished 5th in Division Two							
09/05/51	Rapid Vienna	H	FoB*	2-2	9	18,000	
12/05/51	Bradford City	H	WRSC	0-4	9	15,000	
14/05/51	FC Haarlem	H	FoB	2-0	5	9,362	
*Festival of Britain							

KING JOHN

John Charles's Career At Leeds United

DATE	OPPONENT	H/A	COMP	SCORE	NO	ATT	GOALS
1951-52 Season							
01/12/51	Swansea T	H	Lge 2	1-1	5	26,235	
08/12/51	Coventry City	A	Lge 2	2-4	5	14,621	
15/12/51	Brentford	A	Lge 2	1-2	5	17,957	
22/12/51	Doncaster Rvrs	H	Lge 2	0-0	5	21,793	
25/12/51	Leicester City	A	Lge 2	2-1	5	24,498	
26/12/51	Leicester City	H	Lge 2	2-1	5	29,422	
29/12/51	Everton	A	Lge 2	0-2	5	37,616	
05/01/52	Southampton	H	Lge 2	1-1	5	25,319	
12/01/52	Rochdale	A	FAC3	2-0	5	21,475	
19/01/52	Sheffield Wed	A	Lge 2	2-1	5	42,354	
26/01/52	West Ham Utd	H	Lge 2	3-1	5	32,297	
02/02/52	Bradford	H	FAC4	2-0	5	50,645	
09/02/52	Rotherham	A	Lge 2	3-0	5	47,985	
16/02/52	Sheffield Utd	A	Lge 2	0-3	5	36,265	
23/02/52	Chelsea	H	FAC4	1-1	5	52,328	
27/02/52	Chelsea	A	FAC4R	1-1aet	5	60,851	
01/03/52	Barnsley	H	Lge 2	1-0	5	32,221	
03/03/52	Chelsea	N*	FAC4R	1-5	5	30,504	
played at Villa Park							
22/03/52	QPR	A	Lge 2	0-0	5	15,195	
05/04/52	Luton T	A	Lge 2	1-2	5	11,460	
11/04/52	Nottingham F	A	Lge 2	1-1	9	28,808	
12/04/52	Bury	H	Lge 2	2-1	9	23,004	
14/04/52	Nottingham F	H	Lge 2	0-0	9	26,511	
Leeds finished 6th in Division Two							
1952-53 Season							
23/08/52	Huddersfield T	A	Lge 2	0-1	5	35,230	
28/08/52	Bury	A	Lge 2	2-2	5	12,274	
30/08/52	Plymouth A	H	Lge 2	1-1	5	25,067	
03/09/52	Bury	A	Lge 2	2-0	5	14,623	
06/09/52	Rotherham	A	Lge 2	1-3	5	14,900	
10/09/52	Birmingham City	H	Lge 2	0-1	5	14,133	
13/09/52	Fulham	H	Lge 2	2-0	5	18,371	
17/09/52	Birmingham City	A	Lge 2	2-2	5	18,371	
20/09/52	West Ham Utd	A	Lge 2	2-2	5	22,437	
24/09/52	Southampton	H	Lge 2	1-1	5	13,299	
27/09/52	Leicester City	H	Lge 2	0-1	5	19,724	
04/10/52	Notts County	A	Lge 2	2-3	5	22,836	
08/10/52	Halifax T	H	WRSC	2-1	9	3,500	2
11/10/52	Sheffield Utd	A	Lge 2	1-2	9	33,683	
18/10/52	Barnsley	H	Lge 2	4-1	9	22,155	1
25/10/52	Lincoln City	A	Lge 2	1-1	9	15,491	1
01/11/52	Hull City	H	Lge 2	3-1	9	25,538	3
08/11/52	Blackburn Rvrs	A	Lge 2	1-1	9	22,510	1
22/11/52	Everton	A	Lge 2	2-2	9	28,664	2
29/11/52	Brentford	H	Lge 2	3-2	9	16,077	3
06/12/52	Doncaster Rvrs	A	Lge 2	0-0	9	15,744	
13/12/52	Swansea T	H	Lge 2	5-1	9	21,065	2 (1pen)
20/12/52	Huddersfield T	H	Lge 2	2-1	9	34,365	1
26/12/52	Luton T	A	Lge 2	0-2	9	19,480	
27/12/52	Luton T	H	Lge 2	2-2	9	31,634	1
03/01/53	Plymouth A	A	Lge 2	1-0	9	27,149	
10/01/53	Brentford	A	FAC3	1-2	9	22,650	1
17/01/53	Rotherham	H	Lge 2	4-0	9	24,048	3
24/01/53	Fulham	A	Lge 2	1-2	9	21,210	
07/02/53	West Ham Utd	H	Lge 2	3-2	9	17,680	2

DATE	OPPONENT	H/A	COMP	SCORE	NO	ATT	GOALS
14/02/53	Leicester City	A	Lge 2	3-3	9	21,754	2
21/02/53	Notts County	H	Lge 2	3-1	9	22,922	
28/02/53	Sheffield Utd	H	Lge 2	0-3	9	39,858	
07/03/53	Barnsley	A	Lge 2	2-2	9	11,536	1
14/03/53	Lincoln City	H	Lge 2	2-1	9	18,293	
21/03/53	Hull City	A	Lge 2	0-1	9	25,387	
28/03/53	Blackburn Rvrs	H	Lge 2	0-0	9	10,644	
11/04/53	Everton	H	Lge 2	2-0	8	15,363	
16/04/53	Swansea T	A	Lge 2	2-3	9	21,262	1
18/04/53	Brentford	A	Lge 2	3-3	8	12,703	2
22/04/53	Nottingham F	H	Lge 2	2-1	8	11,497	
25/04/53	Doncaster Rvrs	H	Lge 2	1-1	9	12,715	
1953-54 Season							
19/08/53	Notts County	H	Lge 2	6-0	9	18,432	4
22/08/53	Rotherham Utd	H	Lge 2	4-2	9	24,309	3
27/08/53	Swansea T	A	Lge 2	3-4	9	26,408	1
29/08/53	Leicester City	A	Lge 2	0-3	9	21,984	
02/09/53	Swansea T	H	Lge 2	3-2	9	20,949	2
05/09/53	Stoke City	H	Lge 2	1-1	9	27,571	1
07/09/53	Plymouth A	A	Lge 2	1-1	9	20,356	1
12/09/53	Fulham	A	Lge 2	3-1	9	26,044	2
16/09/53	Plymouth A	H	Lge 2	1-1	9	20,621	
19/09/53	West Ham Utd	H	Lge 2	1-2	9	28,635	1
26/09/53	Leicester City	A	Lge 2	0-2	9	17,979	
03/10/53	Birmingham City	A	Lge 2	3-3	9	26,434	1
17/10/53	Brentford	A	Lge 2	1-2	9	18,329	1

DATE	OPPONENT	H/A	COMP	SCORE	NO	ATT	GOALS
08/09/54	Stoke City	H	Lge 2	0-1	5	20,295	
11/09/54	Swansea T	H	Lge 2	5-2	5	20,040	
13/09/54	Stoke City	A	Lge 2	1-0	5	19,311	
18/09/54	Nottingham F	H	Lge 2	1-1	5	22,402	
02/10/54	Birmingham City	H	Lge 2	1-0	5	21,200	
09/10/54	Derby County	A	Lge 2	4-2	5	20,214	
23/10/54	Bristol Rvrs	A	Lge 2	1-5	9	24,568	
30/10/54	Plymouth A	H	Lge 2	3-2	5	20,613	
06/11/54	Port Vale	A	Lge 2	1-0	5	16,062	
13/11/54	Doncaster Rvrs	H	Lge 2	1-0	5	15,757	
20/11/54	Notts County	A	Lge 2	2-1	5	14,519	
27/11/54	Liverpool	H	Lge 2	2-2	5	22.263	1 (pen)
04/12/54	Blackburn Rvrs	A	Lge 2	2-1	5	26,187	
11/12/54	Fulham	H	Lge 2	1-1	5	30,714	1
18/12/54	Hull City	H	Lge 2	3-0	5	23,991	
25/12/54	Middlesbrough	H	Lge 2	1-1	5	26,344	
27/12/54	Middlesbrough	A	Lge 2	0-1	5	45,271	
01/01/55	Lincoln City	A	Lge 2	0-2	5	12,231	
08/01/55	Torquay Utd	H	FAC£	2-2	9	28,150	1
12/01/55	Torquay Utd	A	FAC3R	0-4	9	12,000	
15/01/55	Bury	H	Lge 2	1-0	5	8,594	
22/01/55	Swansea T	A	Lge 2	0-2	5	19,637	
05/02/55	Nottingham F	A	Lge 2	1-1	5	14,074	1
12/02/55	Ipswich T	H	Lge 2	4-1	5	12,038	
26/02/55	Derby County	H	Lge 2	1-0	5	16,994	1 (pen)
02/03/55	Birmingham City	A	Lge 2	0-2	5	10,774	
05/03/55	West Ham Utd	A	Lge 2	1-2	5	19,664	
12/03/55	Bristol Rvrs	H	Lge 2	2-0	5	16,922	
19/03/55	Plymouth A	A	Lge 2	1-3	5	19,968	
26/03/55	Port Vale	H	Lge 2	3-0	5	8,831	1 (pen)
02/04/55	Doncaster Rvrs	A	Lge 2	1-0	5	12,740	
08/04/55	Luton T	A	Lge 2	0-0	5	25,775	
09/04/55	Notts County	H	Lge 2	2-0	5	24,564	
11/04/55	Luton T	H	Lge 2	4-0	5	29,583	2 (2pen)
16/04/55	Liverpool	A	Lge 2	2-2	5	34,950	
23/04/55	Blackburn Rvrs	H	Lge 2	2-0	5	39,208	
30/04/55	Fulham	A	Lge 2	3-1	5	21,400	

Leeds finished 4th in Division Two

08/05/55	Bradford	H	WRSC	2-1	5	4,000	

1955-56 Season

20/08/55	Barnsley	A	Lge 2	1-2	5	19,341	
22/08/55	Bury	H	Lge 2	1-0	5	19,722	
27/08/55	Middlesbrough	H	Lge 2	2-0	5	22,535	
30/08/55	Bury	A	Lge 2	0-1	5	11,674	
03/09/55	Bristol City	A	Lge 2	1-0	5	31,060	
05/09/55	Hull City	H	Lge 2	1-0	5	17,524	
10/09/55	West Ham Utd	H	Lge 2	3-3	5	21,855	
17/09/55	Port Vale	A	Lge 2	0-2	5	21,348	
24/09/55	Rotherham Utd	A	Lge 2	4-1	4	23,763	
01/10/55	Swansea T	A	Lge 2	1-1	4	29,477	
08/10/55	Nottingham F	H	Lge 2	3-0	4	21,272	1
15/10/55	Sheffield Wed	A	Lge 2	0-4	4	27,640	
29/10/55	Bristol Rvrs	A	Lge 2	1-4	9	24,575	
05/11/55	Stoke City	H	Lge 2	1-0	9	21,261	1
12/11/55	Plymouth A	A	Lge 2	3-4	9	19,122	1
19/11/55	Liverpool	H	Lge 2	4-2	9	22,596	2
26/11/55	Leicester City	A	Lge 2	2-5	9	30,196	2 (2pen)

24/10/53	Derby County	H	Lge 2	3-1	9	26,430	2
31/10/53	Blackburn Rvrs	A	Lge 2	2-2	9	25,272	
07/11/53	Doncaster Rvrs	H	Lge 2	3-1	9	26,830	
14/11/53	Bury	A	Lge 2	4-4	9	11,915	3
28/11/53	Everton	A	Lge 2	1-2	9	55,970	1
05/12/53	Hull City	H	Lge 2	0-0	9	21,070	
12/12/53	Notts County	A	Lge 2	0-2	9	17,552	
19/12/53	Rotherham Utd	H	Lge 2	4-2	9	13,145	3 (1pen)
25/12/53	Nottingham F	A	Lge 2	2-5	9	19,725	1
26/12/53	Nottingham F	H	Lge 2	0-2	9	22,135	
02/01/54	Leicester City	H	Lge 2	7-1	9	21,532	1
09/01/54	Tottenham H	H	FAC3	3-3	9	41,465	1
13/01/54	Tottenham H	A	FAC3R	0-1	9	35,023	
16/01/54	Stoke City	A	Lge 2	0-4	9	26,794	
23/01/54	Fulham	H	Lge 2	1-2	9	20,170	1
06/02/54	West Ham Utd	A	Lge 2	2-5	9	15,585	
13/02/54	Lincoln City	H	Lge 2	5-2	9	15,325	3
20/02/54	Birmingham City	H	Lge 2	1-1	9	22,803	
27/02/54	Bristol Rvrs	A	Lge 2	1-1	9	26,846	
06/03/54	Brentford	H	Lge 2	4-0	9	16,501	2
15/03/54	Huddersfield T	H	WRSC	2-1	9	23,000	1
20/03/54	Blackburn Rvrs	H	Lge 2	3-2	9	24,915	1 (pen)
27/03/54	Oldham Ath	A	Lge 2	2-4	9	18,067	1
03/04/54	Everton	H	Lge 2	3-1	9	22,581	
10/04/54	Doncaster Rvrs	A	Lge 2	0-0	9	12,472	
16/04/54	Luton T	A	Lge 2	1-1	9	16,129	1
17/04/54	Bury	H	Lge 2	3-4	9	17,156	2 (1pen)
19/04/54	Luton T	H	Lge 2	2-1	9	13,930	2 (1pen)
24/04/54	Hull City	A	Lge 2	1-1	9	18,619	1

Leeds finished 10th in Division Two

1954-55 Season

21/08/54	Hull City	A	Lge 2	2-0	9	32,071	1
25/08/54	Rotherham Utd	H	Lge 2	2-4	9	25,021	2
28/08/54	Lincoln City	A	Lge 2	2-3	9	22,326	
30/08/54	Rotherham Utd	A	Lge 2	0-3	9	17,799	
04/09/54	Bury	A	Lge 2	3-5	9	15,357	1

KING JOHN

John Charles's Career At Leeds United

DATE	OPPONENT	H/A	COMP	SCORE	NO	ATT	GOALS
28/11/55	Huddersfield T	H	WRSC	5-2	9	12,500	4
03/12/55	Doncaster Rvrs	H	Lge 2	3-0	9	21,769	1
10/12/55	Blackburn Rvrs	A	Lge 2	3-2	9	18,898	2 (1pen)
17/12/55	Barnsley	H	Lge 2	3-1	9	23,493	
24/12/55	Middlesbrough	A	Lge 2	3-5	9	19,416	1
26/12/55	Notts County	H	Lge 2	1-0	9	24,869	
27/12/55	Notts County	A	Lge 2	1-2	9	23,910	1
31/12/55	Bristol City	H	Lge 2	2-1	9	31,751	
07/01/56	Cardiff City	H	FAC3	1-2	5	40,000	
14/01/56	West Ham Utd	A	Lge 2	1-1	9	20,000	1
21/01/56	Port Vale	H	Lge 2	1-1	9	23,680	
11/02/56	Swansea T	H	Lge 2	2-2	9	20,089	1 (pen)
25/02/56	Sheffield Wed	H	Lge 2	2-1	8	43,268	1
28/02/56	Liverpool	A	Lge 2	0-1	8	21,068	
03/03/56	Lincoln City	A	Lge 2	1-1	8	13,713	1 (pen)
10/03/56	Blackburn Rvrs	H	Lge 2	1-2	8	28,380	1
17/03/56	Stoke City	A	Lge 2	1-2	8	22,784	
24/03/56	Plymouth A	H	Lge 2	4-2	8	12,348	2
30/03/56	Fulham	A	Lge 2	2-1	8	25,459	1
31/03/56	Nottingham F	A	Lge 2	0-2	8	19,448	
02/04/56	Fulham	H	Lge 2	6-1	8	20,115	3
07/04/56	Leicester City	H	Lge 2	4-0	8	26,408	2 (1pen)
14/04/56	Doncaster Rvrs	A	Lge 2	2-1	8	18,404	1
21/04/56	Bristol Rvrs	H	Lge 2	2-1	8	49,274	1
23/04/56	Rotherham Utd	A	Lge 2	2-0	8	20,013	
28/04/56	Hull City	A	Lge 2	4-1	8	31,123	2 (1pen)

Leeds finished 2nd in Division Two

1956-57 Season

DATE	OPPONENT	H/A	COMP	SCORE	NO	ATT	GOALS
18/08/56	Everton	H	Lge 1	5-1	8	31,379	1
23/08/56	Charlton Ath	A	Lge 1	2-1	8	23,299	2
25/08/56	Tottenham H	A	Lge 1	1-5	8	51,212	
29/08/56	Charlton Ath	H	Lge 1	4-0	8	34,444	1
01/09/56	Chelsea	H	Lge 1	0-0	8	38,679	
05/09/56	Manchester City	A	Lge 1	0-1	8	34,185	
08/09/56	Bolton W	H	Lge 1	3-2	8	40,010	1
12/09/56	Manchester City	H	Lge 1	2-0	8	35,068	1
15/09/56	Wolves	A	Lge 1	2-1	8	40,824	2
22/09/56	Aston Villa	H	Lge 1	1-0	8	35,388	1
29/09/56	Luton T	A	Lge 1	2-2	8	20,949	2
06/10/56	Cardiff City	A	Lge 1	1-4	8	38,333	
13/10/56	Birmingham City	H	Lge 1	1-1	8	34,460	
03/11/56	Newcastle Utd	A	Lge 1	3-2	8	49,034	1
10/11/56	Sheffield Wed	H	Lge 1	3-1	8	31,857	3
17/11/56	Manchester Utd	A	Lge 1	2-3	8	52,401	1 (pen)
24/11/56	Arsenal	H	Lge 1	3-3	8	39,113	2
26/11/56	Halifax T	H	WRSC	3-1	8	3,500	
01/12/56	West Brom	H	Lge 1	0-0	8	29,000	
08/12/56	Portsmouth	H	Lge 1	4-1	8	29,866	2
15/12/56	Everton	A	Lge 1	1-2	8	33,765	
25/12/56	Blackpool	A	Lge 1	1-1	8	20,517	
26/12/56	Blackpool	H	Lge 1	5-0	8	22,689	2
29/12/56	Chelsea	A	Lge 1	1-1	8	43,860	
05/01/57	Cardiff City	H	FAC3	1-2	8	34,237	1
12/01/57	Bolton W	A	Lge 1	3-5	8	25,705	2
19/01/57	Wolves	H	Lge 1	0-0	8	32,910	
02/02/57	Aston Villa	A	Lge 1	1-1	8	39,432	
09/02/57	Luton T	H	Lge 1	1-2	8	25,646	1

DATE	OPPONENT	H/A	COMP	SCORE	NO	ATT	GOALS
16/02/57	Cardiff City	H	Lge 1	3-0	8	21,695	1
23/02/57	Preston N E	A	Lge 1	0-3	8	14,036	
02/03/57	Tottenham H	H	Lge 1	1-1	8	33,895	1
09/03/57	Portsmouth	A	Lge 1	5-2	9	23,596	2
11/03/57	Burnley	H	Lge 1	1-1	9	31,956	1
16/03/57	Newcastle Utd	H	Lge 1	0-0	9	32,541	
26/03/57	Sheffield Wed	A	Lge 1	3-2	9	33,205	3
30/03/57	Manchester Utd	H	Lge 1	1-2	9	47,216	1
06/04/57	Arsenal	A	Lge 1	0-1	9	40,388	
13/04/57	West Brom	H	Lgc 1	0 0	9	20,905	
19/04/57	Sunderland	A	Lge 1	0-2	9	56,551	
20/04/57	Birmingham City	A	Lge 1	2-6	9	30,642	2
22/04/57	Sunderland	H	Lge 1	3-1	9	29,328	2

Leeds finished 8th in Division One
John Charles signed for Juventus for £65,000 in May 1957

1962-63 Season

DATE	OPPONENT	H/A	COMP	SCORE	NO	ATT	GOALS
18/08/62	Stoke City	A	Lge 2	1-0	9	27,118	
22/08/62	Rotherham Utd	H	Lge 2	3-4	9	14,119	1
25/08/62	Sunderland	H	Lge 2	1-0	9	17,753	
28/08/62	Rotherham Utd	A	Lge 2	1-2	9	19,508	1
01/09/62	Huddersfield T	A	Lge 2	1-1	9	34,946	1
05/09/62	Bury	H	Lge 2	1-2	9	28,313	
15/09/62	Chelsea	H	Lge 2	2-0	9	27,520	
18/09/62	Bury	A	Lge 2	1-3	9	18,876	
29/09/62	Southampton	H	Lge 2	1-1	9	25,408	
06/10/62	Middlesbrough	H	Lge 2	2-3	4	28,222	
13/10/62	Derby County	A	Lge 2	0-0	9	14,246	

John Charles signed for Roma for £70,000 October 1962